early Listening Skills for Children with a Hearing Loss

Now in a revised and updated second edition, *Early Listening Skills* is a practical manual for use with children and young people with underdeveloped listening skills related to hearing loss. Thirteen clear and easy to follow sections focus on skills such as auditory detection, discrimination, recognition, sequencing and memory. Each one is filled with a series of carefully designed activities to stimulate and develop auditory awareness and discrimination skills in children with a range of developmental levels and abilities.

Features include:

- A wide range of activities suited to both the early years and home settings
- Links to the Early Years Foundation Stage (EYFS) framework and topics reflecting the EYFS and Key Stage 1 curriculum
- Photocopiable material designed to document the child's development over time

As most of the activities are non-verbal, they are well suited for children with limited spoken language as well as children with special educational needs and disability and English as an additional language (EAL) learners. Whilst primarily designed for early years practitioners, special educational needs co-ordinators (SENCOs), specialist teachers, therapists and other professionals, the activity sheets and guidance also make it an invaluable tool for parents and caregivers looking to stimulate listening skills at home.

Diana Williams qualified as a Speech and Language Therapist in 1983, and worked in schools and nurseries with children who have communication difficulties. She developed a specialist knowledge in the field of hearing loss, and completed an MSc in Speech Therapy with Deaf People at City University, London, in 1992. Her other publications include the companion volume *Early Visual Skills* and the popular *Working with Children's Language*. In 2002, she authored a word finding and categorising game named 'Find the Link' for individuals and group work. In addition to her clinical roles, Diana held a number of lecturing posts in higher education institutions, teaching and supporting a diverse range of students. After gaining a Postgraduate Diploma in Education in 2004, she provided professional development activities for other lecturers and teachers as an Educational Developer. More recently she completed a BA(Hons) in Fine Art and a MA in Fine Art, and now focuses her time on arts education and arts practice.

early Listening Skills for Children with a Hearing Loss

A Resource for Professionals in Health and Education

Second Edition

Diana Williams

LONDON AND NEW YORK

Second edition published 2020
by Routledge
2 Park Square, Milton Park, Abingdon, Oxon, OX14 4RN

and by Routledge
52 Vanderbilt Avenue, New York, NY 10017

Routledge is an imprint of the Taylor & Francis Group, an informa business

© 2020 Diana Williams

The right of Diana Williams to be identified as author of this work has been asserted by her in accordance with sections 77 and 78 of the Copyright, Designs and Patents Act 1988.

All rights reserved. The purchase of this copyright material confers the right on the purchasing institution to photocopy pages which bear the photocopy icon and copyright line at the bottom of the page. No other part of this publication may be reproduced, stored in a retrieval system, or transmitted in any form or by any means, electronic, mechanical, photocopying, recording or otherwise, without prior permission in writing from the publisher.

Trademark notice: Product or corporate names may be trademarks or registered trademarks, and are used only for identification and explanation without intent to infringe.

First edition published by Speechmark, 1995

British Library Cataloguing-in-Publication Data
A catalogue record for this book is available from the British Library

Library of Congress Cataloging-in-Publication Data
Names: Williams, Diana, 1957- author.
Title: Early listening skills for children with a hearing loss : a resource for professionals in health and education / Diana Williams.
Other titles: Early listening skills
Description: Second edition. | Abingdon, Oxon ; New York, NY : Routledge, 2020. | Series: Early skills | First edition published under title: Early listening skills. Bicester : Winslow, 1995. | Includes bibliographical references.
Identifiers: LCCN 2019025075 (print) | LCCN 2019025076 (ebook) | ISBN 9780367193461 (paperback) | ISBN 9780429201912 (ebook)
Subjects: LCSH: Hearing impaired children—Education (Early childhood) | Deaf children—Education (Early childhood) | Listening—Study and teaching (Early childhood)—Activity programs. | Hearing disorders in children—Treatment.
Classification: LCC HV2443.W55 2020 (print) | LCC HV2443 (ebook) | DDC 371.91/2—dc23
LC record available at https://lccn.loc.gov/2019025075
LC ebook record available at https://lccn.loc.gov/2019025076

ISBN: 978-0-367-19346-1 (pbk)
ISBN: 978-0-429-20191-2 (ebk)

Typeset in Times New Roman
by Apex CoVantage, LLC

Please note that in this text 'she' is used to refer to the child for the sake of clarity alone.

EARLY LISTENING SKILLS
Contents

	Acknowledgements	◆ vi
	Introduction	◆ vii
SECTION 1	*Discovering Sound*	◆ 1
SECTION 2	*Exploring Sound Makers*	◆ 11
SECTION 3	*Sound Detection*	◆ 23
SECTION 4	*Sound Recognition*	◆ 47
SECTION 5	*Finding Sound*	◆ 75
SECTION 6	*Volume and Pitch*	◆ 105
SECTION 7	*Rhythm and Sequencing*	◆ 123
SECTION 8	*Auditory Memory*	◆ 147
SECTION 9	*Listening to Spoken Language*	◆ 163
SECTION 10	*Listening Skills in the Curriculum*	◆ 195
SECTION 11	*Holiday Projects*	◆ 201
SECTION 12	*Listening Resources*	◆ 209
SECTION 13	*Sounds, Sound Makers and Musical Instruments*	◆ 219
APPENDIX I	*Record Sheet*	◆ 243
APPENDIX II	*Further Reading*	◆ 244
APPENDIX III	*Resources*	◆ 245

ACKNOWLEDGEMENTS

This book would not have been possible without the support and encouragement of friends and colleagues. I would particularly like to express my appreciation to the children and families with whom I have worked and who have provided inspiration and motivation for this project.

INTRODUCTION

Early Listening Skills is a photocopiable resource intended for use by health and education professionals who are working with children who have underdeveloped listening skills related to hearing loss. The activities are designed to stimulate and develop auditory awareness and auditory discrimination skills. Children with a hearing loss have an obvious disadvantage in developing these skills, as auditory information may be distorted or not audible.

The majority of the activities are non-verbal and are therefore suitable for children with limited spoken language or as an early participatory activity for children who have English as an additional language (EAL). They are primarily aimed at children in early years and Key Stage 1 (KS1) but may also be suitable for older children with special educational needs and disability (SEND). In addition, activities can be modified to suit the needs of a range of children who need support with their listening and attention skills.

Practitioners, parents and carers intending to use these activities should always consult appropriate specialists. The needs of the specific child will dictate who would be the best advisor. However, they would probably include some of the following: teachers of the deaf, educational audiologists, specialist speech and language therapists, special educational needs (SEN) teachers and occupational therapists.

HOW THE ACTIVITIES ARE ORGANIZED

Sections 1–7 of the book cover the skills of auditory awareness, sound detection, sound recognition, auditory discrimination and sequencing. Section 8 has guidance on auditory memory strategies and specific listening activities. Section 9 addresses listening to spoken language in the form of single words, simple commands and complex commands. Additional sections (10–12) describe topics for the curriculum, holiday projects and listening resources. The final section (13) provides a comprehensive list of sounds, sound makers and musical instruments.

Sections 1–10 provide teaching guidelines or specific teaching activities designed to promote the development of the target listening skill. Activity sheets are provided for each auditory skill area. The activity sheets for early years settings can be photocopied and distributed to other practitioners supporting the child's learning and development. Photocopiable activity sheets are also provided for home so that parents and carers can reinforce learning and help to generalize skills.

HOW TO USE THE ACTIVITIES

It is essential that activities are compatible with the child's developmental level, particularly their auditory skills, language and communication abilities. The introduction to each section will help the user to decide whether the child is ready for a particular stage or needs less advanced activities. Some listening skills, such as sequencing sound and listening to speech, can be worked on simultaneously. Others follow a strict developmental sequence; for example, the child must be able to detect a sound before she can learn to recognize it. The choice of activities will also depend on the individual child.

Teaching activity

Sections 3–7 and 9 have several teaching activities that provide a detailed model for teaching a particular skill. Although these are for individual children, they can easily be adapted for groups.

Useful words and phrases

A list of words and phrases has been included with each teaching activity, which may be spoken and/or signed as appropriate to the individual child's needs and preferences. These examples are intended only as a guideline, which the user may choose to omit, as it is possible to demonstrate the expected responses to the child non-verbally in many of the activities. Alternatively, the user may decide to substitute other words or phrases, which are more suited to the language and cultural needs of the individual child. However, the consistent use of language will provide structure to the activity and reinforce language development.

Increasing the complexity of the activity

Advice is provided on how the complexity of each teaching activity can be increased. These suggestions can be used to adapt the activity to the needs of the individual child and provide ideas for teachers on differentiation.

Variations

A list of variations is included with each teaching activity. It has suggestions for similar activities and ideas on how to vary the teaching activity to satisfy the child's interests. These have a variety of developmental levels, so the adult needs to be aware of the child's overall capabilities when selecting alternative games. For example, an activity using picture material is developmentally more advanced for the child than one using large objects.

Activities sheets for early years settings

Activities sheets for early years settings are provided for each area of listening skills. The activities on these sheets include structured activities aimed at supporting the child's learning of specific listening skills and generalization activities to reinforce this learning and support the early years curriculum. There is a range of activities that can be easily adapted for use with individual children, children working together in a pair or for small groups of children.

Early years practitioners, SENCOs, specialist teachers, specialist therapists or other relevant professionals, in consultation with the parent or carer, can select activities appropriate for early years settings by ticking the check box. For example:

 Mark a pattern
Give the child some paint markers and some paper. Ask her to make a mark each time you play a beat on a drum.

The following considerations should be borne in mind when selecting activities:

- the auditory, cognitive, linguistic and developmental needs of the child;
- the child's everyday routines;
- the child's educational curriculum;
- the child's interests, likes and dislikes:
- the availability of materials;
- the support staff's preference for activities.

Activities sheets for parents

Activities sheets for use at home are provided for each area of listening skills. They provide practical advice on how to use the child's everyday routines to stimulate auditory awareness and suggest games to develop the child's auditory perceptual skills.

The majority of the activities are for one-to-one play with a parent, other family member or carer. They are also appropriate for other care providers in early years settings, like child minders, who may need to support individual children. There are some suggestions for group activities, which could be played as a party game or with the child's friends.

Early years practitioners, SENCOs, specialist teachers, specialist therapists or other relevant professionals, in consultation with the parent or carer, can select activities appropriate for the home by ticking the check box. For example:

 Hide the music
Play hiding games with your child. Use a musical instrument like a drum or rattle and hide with it somewhere in the room. Make a continuous or repetitive sound. Can your child find you by listening for that sound?

The following considerations should be borne in mind when selecting activities:

- the auditory, cognitive, linguistic and developmental needs of the child;
- the child's everyday routines;
- the social and cultural context of the child;
- the child's interests, likes and dislikes;
- the availability of materials;
- the parent or carer's preference for activities.

These considerations should be discussed with the family, and activities should be explained and demonstrated if possible. The aim is for the family and child to enjoy the experience of playing and learning together.

Materials and equipment

A list of suitable materials, toys and equipment is provided for each area of auditory perceptual skill where appropriate, along with suggestions for sounds and sound makers. These items have been selected as the most relevant for the activities in a particular section and should be used in conjunction with the corresponding activities sheet. They include standard educational equipment, musical instruments, everyday objects, toys, games and homemade items. Objects, toys and homemade items provide an opportunity to link activities with the cultural experience of the child. The list can also be used to stimulate ideas for adapting and extending activities and games. Using a variety of material in this way will help the child to generalize her skills.

Advice should be sought on the suitability of the equipment and materials for individual children from relevant health and education professionals, as the child's cognitive, perceptual, linguistic and developmental level will determine the choice of materials. For example, sounds and sound makers should be selected in relation to their audibility to the child. (See 'Auditory Stimuli' and 'Materials for Teaching'.)

This section can also be used to identify appropriate items for a specific child. Parents, carers and professionals should be consulted regarding the child's preferences and the availability of items. After discussion, suitable items can be selected with a tick. For example:

A variety of musical instruments or music makers can be used for listening to high and low sounds, for example:

- ☑ metal chime bars
- ☐ wooden chime bars
- ☐ glockenspiel
- ☑ xylophone

The list can be photocopied and distributed to other professionals, parents and carers and should be used in conjunction with the corresponding activities sheet.

CREATING A GOOD LISTENING ENVIRONMENT

A good listening environment that reduces background noise will benefit the learning and attainment of all children. Research has shown that children perform less well in the areas of attention (visual and auditory), memory, problem solving and language-based tasks like reading in a noisy environment. Speech intelligibility is also negatively impacted, with reduced ability in auditory discrimination and speech perception. So it is especially important for children with a hearing loss, who will find it difficult to filter important sounds like speech from background noise.

To create a good listening environment:

Reduce or eliminate background noise

In a learning space like a nursery or classroom, noise might come from children moving, talking, shouting or engaging in active play. Other ambient noise may occur from multimedia equipment, like computers and projectors, or from heating or air-conditioning systems. This may adversely affect the signal to noise ratio, or in other words, how loud a sound is in relation to the background noise, for example, the teacher's voice. A favourable signal to noise ratio (+20dB) is best in optimizing how intelligible the spoken message is for a deaf child. Avoid shouting to achieve this difference; instead, plan how to reduce background noise.

Manage noise levels in the classroom by:

- turning off electrical equipment like projectors when not in use (this will save energy too);
- putting soft pads on chair and table legs to prevent scraping noises;
- lining noisy storage tins, plastic tubs, pots and trays with felt;
- reducing unnecessary classroom chatter;
- introducing quiet times.

Primary teachers might want to consider using a classroom noise monitor app that provides visual feedback on background noise and helps students to monitor their own noise levels. A number of commercial or free apps are available online.

Reduce reverberation or echo

The acoustic quality of a learning space, in terms of how much a sound reverberates or echoes, is another important factor to consider in creating a good listening environment. Reverberation distorts sound and contributes to the overall level of background noise, adversely affecting speech intelligibility for a deaf child. Think of how sound echoes in large rooms with high ceilings with little or no soft furnishings. In addition, in this type of environment children and adults may feel the need to raise their voice to be heard over this reverberation, a phenomenon known as the Lombard Effect.

Improve the sound absorbency of hard surfaces by:

- covering display tables, cupboards and desks with fabric;
- hanging curtains or blinds;
- using a fabric background for displays on walls;
- providing soft furnishings like cushions and bean bags;
- hanging mobiles from the ceiling;
- increasing the number of carpeted areas;
- installing specialist acoustic treatments.

Make sure there is good sound insulation

Noise may intrude into the learning space from the corridor or from noisy activities in other rooms like PE or music lessons. External noise from traffic, building or road works may also be a problem.

Prevent intrusive noise by:

- closing doors and windows where possible;
- using blinds or curtains to shut out noise*;
- using displays, especially with sound absorbing material like fabric, in communal areas like corridors and halls.

* Remember the child with a hearing loss needs a well-lit space to see your face, and the faces of the other children, in order to lip-read and see facial expression.

Make an acoustic survey of your learning space to identify possible problem areas and sources of noise. As well as *looking* at your environment, *listen* to a recording of everyday noises, and identify the causes. Use the previous suggestions to remedy any acoustic issues. (See more detailed guidance and resources for acoustic surveys on the National Deaf Children's Society website, www.ndcs.org.uk/acoustics.)

Familiarize yourself with the hearing technologies that help improve listening conditions for deaf children like radio aids, soundfield systems and digital streamers. Seek advice from the teacher of the deaf or educational audiologist, who will be able to offer support and guidance on technologies.

EFFECTIVE COMMUNICATION STRATEGIES

Remember the following strategies when communicating with a child who has a hearing loss:

- get the child's attention before speaking;
- make sure you are on the same eye level as the child;
- make sure your face is well lit (avoid standing or sitting in front of a light source like a window);
- maintain eye contact while speaking (avoid turning away);

Introduction

- avoid covering your mouth when speaking;
- speak clearly with normal intonation (avoid shouting, exaggerating mouth or head movements or talking very slowly).

SETTING UP LEARNING SITUATIONS

Follow these guidelines to make optimum use of the learning situation:

1. Reduce background noise (see the previous section on 'Creating a Good Listening Environment') and visual distractions so that the child or children can concentrate on the listening activity.

2. If you are working in a classroom or a nursery, try to have an uncluttered corner that can be partitioned off. Sit away from environmental sound sources like heating equipment, projectors and computers. This is particularly important for children who have a sensory impairment and who may have difficulties with hearing and vision.

3. Make sure the child is seated in a way that allows her maximum involvement in the activity. She should be able to see, touch and hear equipment and be able to move around easily if required.

4. Seat the child in the best position to see your face for lip reading and at the optimum distance for listening (one metre). Children who have unilateral hearing loss, or deafness in one ear, need to be seated so the speaker is on the side of the hearing ear.

5. Carry out the activities with an adult who is known and liked by the child. She is more likely to co-operate and enjoy the games. A familiar person will also be able to observe and interpret the child's responses.

6. Check that the child is comfortable and ready to participate.

7. Repeat the activities frequently. Constant repetition may be necessary to develop a child's skills. This is especially relevant for children with a hearing loss who need a considerable amount of help in making sense of what they hear.

For group activities

1. Decide how you will seat the children. Think about optimum distance for listening (one metre) and the best position to see your face for lip reading.

2. Seat the children according to how well they work with other children and their own needs and preferences. An active child may attend better if she is seated between two quieter children. A passive child may sit still when at the outside of a semi-circle but will need adult help to make sure she participates.

PLANNING THE ACTIVITIES

Use ongoing formative assessment to help plan appropriate activities. Record Sheets (see 'Record Sheets') are provided in each section to encourage the use of observation as a basis for identifying the child's learning and development needs. *Development Matters in the Early Years Foundation Stage (EYFS)* provides comprehensive and detailed development statements that practitioners can use to analyze observations and to structure learning opportunities appropriate to the child's developmental level (see 'Appendix II: Further Reading').

Here are some general guidelines on planning activities:

1. Choose activities that are appropriate for the child's auditory, cognitive, developmental and linguistic level. Give the child time to explore and experience materials through child initiated play before introducing more structured learning activities.

2. Use the guidelines on increasing the complexity of the activity to challenge and expand the child's skills. The activities should build on the child's strengths and help to develop her listening skills to expected levels.

3. Decide on the words or phrases that are appropriate to use in the activity. (Select these from the list given for each activity, or substitute other words and phrases that are more suited to the language and cultural needs of the individual child.)

4. Decide on what responses you require from the child during the activity. This will depend on the type of activity but also on the abilities of the child. (See 'Responses from the Child'.)

5. Plan the length of the activity. You need to allow enough time for the child to process auditory information. She may also have a limited concentration span.

6. Get the child's attention before you start speaking. Use instructions that are clear, simple and within the language abilities of the child. The activities can be modified for children who have a limited understanding of spoken language; for example, the required responses can be demonstrated by the adult.

7. Decide which teaching strategies you will employ during the activity. Here are a few examples:

    ◆ *demonstration* – show the child the expected response to the activity, for example, beating a drum;

    ◆ *providing a model* – give the child a model to copy, for example, chime bars on a chime bar step;

    ◆ *shadowing* – you have an identical set of equipment to that of the child, who is then able to copy each step of the task; for example, the child copies you playing fast and slow beats on a drum with her own drum set;

    ◆ *delayed imitation* – provide a model for the child to copy, for example, a rhythmic pattern on rhythm sticks. Can the child repeat the pattern of beats from memory?

- *backchaining* – the adult takes the lead but leaves the child to complete the activity: for example, singing the last word in a song. The child is gradually expected to sing more and more of the words by herself;

- *frontchaining* – the child starts off an activity and the adult completes it; for example, the adult makes the last few sounds to complete a sequence. The child is gradually expected to do more and more of the sequence by herself.

8 Plan how you will prompt the child if she needs help during the activity. Try the following cues:
- repetition of instructions or auditory stimuli;
- demonstration by the adult or another child of the expected response;
- pointing, gentle physical manipulation, gesture or sign;
- removing choices to increase the probability of the child making the correct response.

The reduction in cues and prompts might be one way that the child's learning is gradually extended and challenged.

9 Part of the learning process involves reinforcing correct responses, so plan how you will praise the child and give feedback. Sometimes the repetition of the stimulus is a form of reward in itself: for example, repeating a sound to make a puppet pop out. Always choose to give feedback in a form that the child is likely to understand. If the child is to learn to attach meaning to sound, it is essential that she is aware when she has made an incorrect response. Avoid being too negative. Help the child to respond correctly by repeating the stimuli and using the prompts suggested earlier.

10 Adapt the activity to suit the individual child's level of concentration. Children who have difficulties in listening often have short attention spans.

11 To maintain the child's interest, use the suggested variations and choose different sound makers. Alternatively, ask the child to be the leader in the activities.

AUDITORY STIMULI

Many children have difficulties with listening skills, but those who have a hearing loss are at a particular disadvantage. Sounds may be distorted or inaudible to the child. Therefore, it is very important to select auditory stimuli that are within the hearing range of these children.

A child with a hearing loss may have difficulty in hearing quiet sounds or sounds of a certain frequency. Some children may be sensitive to certain pitches or tones. Check your choice of sounds or sound makers with the child's teacher of the deaf, educational audiologist or specialist speech and language therapist.

MATERIALS FOR TEACHING

Activities may require the use of a variety of equipment, materials and toys. These need to be selected with just as much care as the auditory stimuli. Remember:

1. A balance needs to be maintained between new and familiar material. Too many new things may frighten or bewilder a child or over stimulate her so that she is unable to attend to the task; too many familiar items and she may become bored, making it difficult to maintain her interest.

2. Materials should be appropriate to the child's developmental, cognitive and linguistic level.

3. Toys and materials should be easy for the child to manipulate.

4. The child's interests, preferences and experiences should be taken into account when choosing materials.

5. Toys and materials that are interactive or provide the child with a challenge are more likely to hold her attention. Look for toys that stimulate visual and tactile exploration as well as listening, demonstrate cause and effect or involve problem solving.

6. Suitable materials are suggested at the beginning of each teaching activity. If these are not appropriate for the child, try the list of musical instruments, sounds or materials for more ideas and inspiration.

RESPONSES FROM THE CHILD

When planning activities, you need to consider the responses the child is expected to make to the auditory stimuli and how the child will participate in the activity. Remember:

1. A child may give a variety of responses to auditory stimuli, including the following: eye or pupil widening; blinking; stilling; smiling or some other change in facial expression; turning to locate a sound; looking at an object or event; a change in vocalization (for example, quietening or increased sound production); reaching towards the sound; pointing; body movements (such as jerks); copying actions, using gestures, symbols, signs or spoken language.

2. The activities require children to participate using a variety of means so that even those with limited vocal skills can take an active part by: eye-pointing, looking, touching, picking up a toy or picture, copying an action or sound.

3. Make it clear to the child how you expect her to participate in the activity by explaining or modelling the response.

4. Look for some sort of novel response from the child. Some responses are open to misinterpretation, so you should look for

patterns and consistencies before deciding whether a child is actually responding to sound in an activity.

5 Be aware of responses that indicate the child is confused or misunderstanding and modify the activity accordingly.

6 The desired responses should be within the range of the child's overall capabilities, not just her auditory skills: for example, if a child is expected to turn and look for a sound, how good is her head control and sight? The other areas to consider are physical, visual, cognitive, linguistic and social skills.

MONITORING THE CHILD'S PROGRESS

Record Sheet

Each section has one or more Record Sheets designed for early years practitioners to complete. The Record Sheet provides a way of recording observations of the child's activities and the child's response to these activities. They are intended to support curriculum planning and provide evidence as to the level of learning and development when reviewing children's progress. It also prompts practitioners to note whether the activity is child initiated or adult initiated.

One example is provided for guidance at the top of each sheet. It is useful to make a note of the following information:

- *describe the activity or context* – name of the activity or a brief description;
- *type of activity* – the area of listening skills being focused on, such as sound recognition;
- *equipment* – sound makers, musical instruments and other materials used in the activity;
- *teaching strategies* – describe the teaching strategies employed in presenting the activity, for example, demonstration;
- *type of interaction:*

    - individual - the child is engaged in an activity alone;
    - pair - the child is engaged in a shared activity with one other child;
    - group - the child is engaged in a small group or class activity;

- *organization of the activity:* where it takes place, who is involved, any special arrangements;
- *observations of the child:* describe what you can see and hear. Focus on what the child can do by herself, as well as what she can do with prompts or help from the adult or other children.
- *language and communication:* make a note of vocabulary used, language in relation to the task and communication with others.

Making a record of your observations forms part of a range of ways you might document a child's development. Remember to include (with the permission of the parent or guardian) - photographs, audio, video and electronic recordings, examples of children's work and information from parents. Children should also be encouraged to communicate about and review their own learning.

SUMMARY OF ESSENTIAL POINTS

- Reduce background noise and visual distractions.
- Use clear speech with normal intonation patterns.
- Position the child to allow for lip reading.
- Use appropriate language levels and familiar vocabulary.
- Use sound makers within the hearing range of the child.
- Look for consistent responses.
- Take into account the child's interests and preferences.
- Be aware of safety considerations.

Introduction

HINTS FOR PARENTS

How to help your child's listening skills

1. Only use sounds or sound makers your child can hear. A teacher of the deaf or speech and language therapist can help you choose the best sounds for your child.

2. Activities should be fun for you and your child. If it seems like hard work, stop! You may need to try again at a different time or change the activity.

3. Help your child to concentrate by keeping background noise quiet; for example, switch off the television or radio.

4. Remember that your child may not get it right the first time. As long as your child is not bored, you can repeat activities as many times as you like.

5. You and your child will not be good playmates if you are hungry or sleepy. Choose a time that suits you as well as your child.

6. Make sure your child can see and hear you by sitting on the same level and near to your child.

7. Do not worry if your child seems to lose interest quickly. Listening can be tiring for some children; several short play sessions are better than one long one.

SECTION 1
Discovering Sound

Introduction *3*

    Teaching Guidelines *4*

    Activities for Early Years Settings *5*

    Activities for Home *7*

    Nursery Rhymes and Songs *9*

Record Sheet *10*

INTRODUCTION

C*hildren enjoy* listening to the noises and speech in their everyday environment and from an early age get pleasure from making their own sounds of gurgles, cries and babble. However, some children may need help in attending to the many sounds that surround them. This is particularly so for children with a hearing loss, who may need help to become aware of the sounds that are a natural part of everyday activities. These activities are important opportunities for the child to learn about sound and gradually make a connection between sounds and actions, objects and events.

The activities in this section are designed to increase the child's awareness of sound in their everyday environment and to engage in reciprocal games, rhymes and songs. There is no specific teaching activity for this section. Instead, guidelines are provided on ways to help the child to be aware of the sounds in their everyday environment.

DISCOVERING SOUND
Teaching Guidelines

It is important that the child has an opportunity to hear and listen to a variety of sounds, noises and vocalizations around her during the day. Encourage the child to notice and attend to these sounds by:

- *staying child focused* – respond to her interests, talk about what she is doing and respond to her communication;
- *being visual* – use facial expression, gesture, actions and body language along with spoken language to attract and maintain the child's attention;
- *using a 'baby' voice* – all adults use this voice to young children. Speech is slower, higher pitched with a singsong rhythm;
- *responding to the child* – talk about what they are doing or copy their vocalizations;
- *making time* – children with a hearing loss may need more time to make connections between sounds and actions or events;
- *using repetition* – children will learn best when games and activities are repeated over and over.

DISCOVERING SOUND
Activities for Early Years Settings

These activities help the child develop an awareness of sound. During the day, vary the child's experience of sound by providing a variety of 'listening environments'. There should be opportunities to listen to sound, to make sound and to have times of quiet.

☐ *Peek-a-boo*

Playing 'Peek-a-boo' is a great way to engage with the child and offers an opportunity for the use of repetitive sounds. Your intonation and facial expression are all part of the game too. For EAL children you may want to find out about similar games the family play at home. These can be learnt and reinforced at nursery.

☐ *Reciprocal songs*

Sing reciprocal songs where the child has to engage in an activity with the adult or another child. For example, passing a beanbag round a circle or rolling a ball to another child. Various rhymes and songs can be adapted to introduce some interactive elements.

☐ *Rhythmic play*

Play songs and games that emphasize rhythm. Try hand-clapping songs like 'pat a cake' and 'if you're happy and you know it'. Or use a drum to beat along with a favourite nursery rhyme.

☐ *Sing a routine*

Songs without music are very useful for a child with a hearing loss, as they can hear the words more clearly without instruments playing in the background. So sing songs during the day to accompany routines like nappy time or lunchtime. Try "This is the way . . ." "Hello, how are you?" Find out from family members what songs are significant for the child at home, and sing these with the child. (There are many examples of songs for daily routines at:
https://www.songsforteaching.com/everyday/everydayroutines.htm)

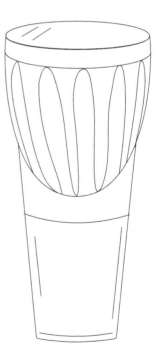

Section 1: Discovering Sound

☐ *Multisensory toys*

Some children with a hearing loss need to learn that sound exists. At first, they may engage with sound through other senses, for example, feeling vibrations. Toys that are interesting to *look at* and *touch* as well as making a *sound* will quickly capture the child's attention, so multisensory toys are an excellent choice. (Available from specialist providers.)

☐ *Treasure baskets*

Collect together some sound makers and some silent toys (teddies, bean bags) for a treasure basket for the child to explore by herself. Make sure to include multisensory toys that have sound, light and offer a tactile experience. (See more suggestions in 'Listening Resources'.)

☐ *Quiet times*

Have some time during the day for quiet times. Here are some ideas: looking at picture books, sticking and gluing, making activities with felt and playdough.

DISCOVERING SOUND
Activities for Home

These activities will help to develop your child's awareness of the sounds around her in everyday life, daily routines and early play.

☐ *Anticipation*

Use sound to help your child anticipate activities; for example, before bath time you could splash the water with your hand as you say "bath time". This will help your child to associate the sound with the activity.

☐ *Daily routines*

Introduce sound play into daily routines like bath time, dinnertime and bedtime.

For example, at bath time show your child how to make a variety of sounds and noises:

- you can splash your hands in the water, or squeeze a wet sponge and let it dribble into the bath;
- use bubble bath for your child to make lots of bubbles by swishing the water;
- sing, "This is the way we wash our hands . . ."
- collect together toys that can be dropped with a plink-plonk into the water;
- there are many cheap wind-up toys in various shapes and sizes that include boats, swimmers and frogs. Your child can wind them up and listen to the noises they make as they flap through the water.

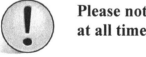 **Please note that water play should be supervised at all times.**

Copyright material from Diana Williams (2020), *Early Listening Skills for Children with a Hearing Loss*, Second Edition, Routledge

Section 1: Discovering Sound

☐ *Everyday sounds*

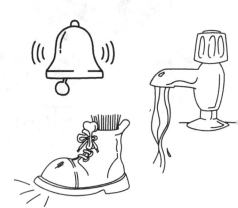

Draw the child's attention to everyday sounds and noises. Let the child see and touch the sound maker if possible and make the sound herself; for example, pressing the doorbell. Reinforce her actions with "You rang the bell – ring ring". Sounds could include the doorbell, footsteps, water running in the sink or a toilet flushing.

☐ *Peek-a-boo*

Playing 'Peek-a-boo' is a great way to engage with your child. Your intonation and facial expression are all part of the game too. Take advantage of everyday situations where her face is momentarily hidden: for example, when dressing her, say "boo!" as she pushes her head through the neck of her jumper.

☐ *Musical toys*

As soon as your child is able to hold a rattle, they are ready to make some musical sounds. Look out for early musical instruments designed specifically for babies like rattles, teether rattles and maraca. As your child gets older choose toys that can be squeezed, shaken or banged together to make a sound. (Check the manufacturer's recommended age range.)

☐ *Lap play*

Sing and talk to your child while she is seated on your lap. You can have fun playing finger games like 'Round and round the garden', 'This little piggy went to market' or rhymes like 'Ride a cock horse to Banbury Cross'. Gently jiggle her up and down to follow the rhythm.

☐ *Singing lullabies*

Singing lullabies to your child is a great way for your child to experience listening to your voice. Choose your favourite ones from childhood. This will also help her to become familiar with the sounds and rhythms of language.

☐ *Action songs*

Sing songs that include lots of actions you can do with your baby. For example, with 'Jack and Jill Went up a Hill', you might walk your fingers up a pretend hill and roll your hands when they come tumbling down. Reinforce your child's responses by imitating any sounds and actions she makes.

DISCOVERING SOUND
Rhymes and Songs

Here are some suggestions for rhymes and action songs that are interactive and encourage an awareness of vocalization:

☐ *Finger rhymes*
- Two little dickie birds
- This little piggy went to market
- Where is thumbkin?
- Round and round the garden
- Fee fi fo fum

☐ *Nursery rhymes*
- Humpty Dumpy sat on a wall
- Five little monkeys
- Baa baa black sheep
- Ride a cock horse to Banbury Cross
- Twinkle, twinkle little star
- Itsy bitsy spider
- Hickory dickory dock
- Hey diddle diddle

☐ *Action Songs*
- Wheels on the bus
- Jack and Jill went up the hill
- I'm a little teapot
- Hokey Cokey
- Row, row, row your boat

Most nursery rhymes can be sung, too!

DISCOVERING SOUND
Record Sheet

Child's name	

Date	Activity/Context	Observations
Example 21.8.	*Played a Peek-a-boo game with the teaching assistant using a scarf from the dressing up box. (AI)*	*Looking in anticipation and giggling when the scarf was dropped to reveal the assistant's face. Copied the word "boo" several times.*

AI = adult initiated activity; CI = child initiated activity

SECTION 2
Exploring Sound Makers

Introduction *13*

    Teaching Guidelines *14*

    Activities for Early Years Settings *15*

    Activities for Home *17*

    Sounds and Sound Makers *21*

Record Sheet *22*

INTRODUCTION

This section has ideas for helping the child to make sounds with a variety of musical instruments and sound makers. The child is encouraged to be an active participant and to explore new and exciting ways of making sounds. The games also involve anticipation and cause and effect.

The activities encourage the child to explore sound makers using sight and touch as well as hearing. Looking at, touching and holding a sound maker will help the child to become more aware of the vibrations and source of the sound. She will learn to anticipate sound and start to make a connection between her own actions and the resulting sounds.

EXPLORING SOUND MAKERS
Teaching Guidelines

Encourage the child to explore a variety of everyday sound makers, musical instruments and her own voice. Allow the child some space and time to initiate her own actions with the sound maker. You can then follow her lead and help to expand her play.

Concentrate on one sound maker at a time. Show the child how one toy can be used to make sound in a variety of ways: for example, a tambourine can be tapped, softly scratched or shaken. Practise the same action on different instruments, so that in one activity the child is shaking a maraca, and in the next one she is shaking sleigh bells.

Use musical instruments and sound makers that provide kinesthetic and tactile feedback. For example, the weight of a pebble in a shaker compared with one filled with rice; or the feel of the vibrations when a large cymbal is struck with a mallet.

Some children may need support from the adult to develop their exploration of sound makers. Below are some ideas on ways to prompt a child to engage with sound makers.

- *modelling* – a child with a hearing loss is more likely to learn by watching and doing;
- *use pauses* – allow time for the child to process what she is seeing, hearing and touching. Let her respond in her own time;
- *playing together* – use a matching sound maker to play alongside the child. Copy the actions and sounds made by the child or join in with her vocalisations;
- *physical prompts* – help the child physically carry out an action: for example, gently pressing her finger down on a button or holding her fingers around a shaker;
- *gesture* – cue the child by miming the appropriate action, or use sign if appropriate.

EXPLORING SOUND MAKERS
Activities for Early Years Settings

To make the most of your sound makers:

- have a special time in the day for children to explore sound makers and musical instruments;
- gather useful items together for a 'listening box' (see p. 213 for ideas);
- try to have pairs of instruments so you can play matching games;
- ask the children's families for ideas about musical instruments and sound makers so that your collection represents various cultures and backgrounds. (This is particularly important for EAL learners.)

Here are some ideas for helping children to explore musical instruments and sound makers.

☐ *Use one sound maker in different ways*

Show the child the different ways sound can be made from one sound maker: for example, a tambourine can be tapped, softly scratched, shaken or hit with the palm of the hand with a soft or hard blow. Strike the back of the tambourine against your knee or thigh, or use a stick to beat out a rhythm.

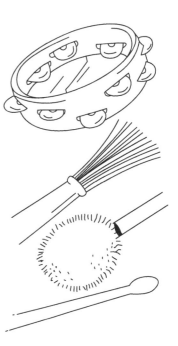

☐ *Make different sounds by using different beaters*

Show the child how different sounds can be made when beaters are varied: for example, the difference between a drum struck by a rubber beater and a drum struck by a wooden beater. Try beaters made out of plastic or ones covered with felt or fabric.

☐ *Make different sounds from different parts of an instrument*

Show the child the different sounds that can be made by using different parts of an instrument: for example, hitting the centre of a cymbal compared with hitting the outer edge.

Section 2: Exploring Sound Makers

☐ *Explore the different volume of sound makers*

Show the child the difference between sound makers that make quiet and loud sounds: for example, Tibetan bells compared with a gong.

Show the child how to make quiet and loud sounds with the same sound maker: for example, banging compared with tapping a drum.

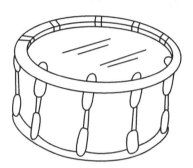

☐ *Explore the different pitch of sound makers*

Show the child the difference in pitch between sound makers: for example, a low-pitched tone bar compared with a high-pitched flute.

Use sound makers like a xylophone to show the difference in pitch on the same instrument.

EXPLORING SOUND MAKERS
Activities for Home

Use toys and everyday objects from around the home to help your child explore a variety of sounds and sound makers.

Make a sound by banging

- ❏ two shells together
- ❏ a wooden spoon on a saucepan
- ❏ two wooden bricks together
- ❏ a wooden spoon on an upside-down tin
- ❏ plastic egg cups together
- ❏ a stick on a box
- ❏ your feet on the ground
- ❏ two saucepan lids together

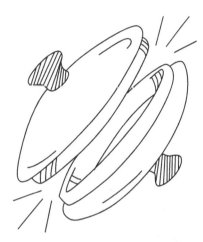

Make a sound by tapping

- ❏ a stick on a fir cone
- ❏ wooden sticks together
- ❏ your fingers on the table or on a tin tray
- ❏ pencils or pens together
- ❏ a stick on an empty plastic bottle
- ❏ a metal spoon on an upturned plastic flower pot

Section 2: Exploring Sound Makers

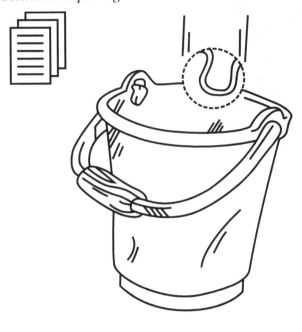

Make a sound by dropping

- a ball into a bucket
- cotton reels into a tin
- toys into the bath
- cutlery onto a tray
- buttons into a jar

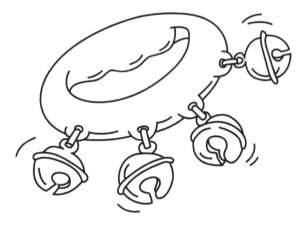

Make a sound by shaking

- a rattle
- your bunch of keys
- a tambourine
- a box of buttons (make sure the lid fits securely)
- a tin of coffee
- toy bricks in an empty box

Make a sound by kicking

- a toy ball with bells inside
- an empty bucket
- your feet through leaves
- a ball against a wall
- a tower of toy bricks

Section 2: Exploring Sound Makers

Make a sound by scrunching

- ☐ stiff paper
- ☐ greaseproof paper
- ☐ tracing paper
- ☐ cellophane
- ☐ wrapping paper
- ☐ bubble wrap

Make a sound by squeezing

- ☐ squeaky toys
- ☐ a horn
- ☐ a hooter
- ☐ a squeeze box

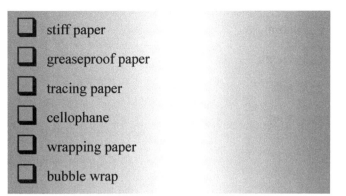

Make a sound by blowing

- ☐ across the opening of an empty bottle (plastic or glass)
- ☐ on tissue paper over a comb
- ☐ a toy trumpet
- ☐ a whistle
- ☐ a raspberry!
- ☐ a mouth organ
- ☐ a paper horn
- ☐ on wind chimes
- ☐ on a musical mobile
- ☐ a kiss

Section 2: Exploring Sound Makers

Make a sound by using your voice to

- ❏ hum
- ❏ laugh
- ❏ talk
- ❏ sing

Encourage your child to copy you. If your child makes a sound or noise, copy her! You can make it into a game by adding a new sound: for example, "bbb" – "bbb boo."

EXPLORING SOUND MAKERS
Sounds and Sound Makers

Here are some suggestions for sound makers that are particularly useful for exploration activities.

- ❏ drum
- ❏ tambourine
- ❏ xylophone
- ❏ chime bars
- ❏ Tibetan bells
- ❏ sleigh bells
- ❏ cymbals
- ❏ gong
- ❏ shakers (egg shakers, maracas)
- ❏ guiro
- ❏ whistle
- ❏ mouth organ
- ❏ flute
- ❏ toy trumpet
- ❏ wind chimes
- ❏ squeaky toys
- ❏ different beaters/mallets (wood, rubber, fabric, felt, plastic)

EXPLORING SOUND MAKERS
Record Sheet

Child's name	

Date	Activity/Context	Observations
Example 20.7.	*Play session with adult in the listening corner using a drum.* (CI)	*Copied tapping a drum with fingers when alongside the adult. Making some babbling sounds.*

AI = adult initiated activity; CI = child initiated activity

SECTION 3
Sound Detection

Introduction 25

Sound or Silence 26

    Teaching Activity 26

    Activities for Early Years Settings 28

    Activities for Home 29

    Musical Instruments and Sound Makers 30

Start and Finish 31

    Teaching Activity 31

    Activities for Early Years Settings 32

    Activities for Home 33

    Musical Instruments and Sound Makers 34

Responding to Sound 35

    Teaching Activity 35

    Activities for Early Years Settings 37

Activities for Home *38*

Sounds and Sound Makers *39*

Symbolic Sounds *40*

Teaching Activity *40*

Activities for Early Years Settings *42*

Activities for Home *43*

Symbolic Sounds *44*

Record Sheet *45*

INTRODUCTION

Children with a hearing loss may have difficulty in detecting sound and distinguishing the start and end of a sound. This section is specifically aimed at developing skills of sound detection in these children. However, other children with listening difficulties will also benefit from these games, which are useful for improving concentration and memory.

The activities include a range of stimuli, from musical instruments to everyday noises and symbolic sounds. This provides an opportunity for the child to experience a variety of sounds produced within appropriate contexts. The activities aim to develop the child's awareness of sound, drawing attention to the start and finish of sounds and developing the child's ability to tell the difference between sound and silence.

It is not necessary for the child to understand what the sound is or even to know whether it is the same as or different from other sounds. Use a variety of sounds, but present only one at a time and avoid making the child have to choose, otherwise the activity will become a sound recognition task.

SOUND DETECTION: SOUND OR SILENCE
Teaching Activity

'Shake the Noise'

You will need:
a wooden brick; two identical tins with removable lids.

Useful words and phrases:
look; listen; tin; brick; shake; noise; silent; lid; empty; full.

What to do:

1. Show the child the two identical tins. Shake each one and then remove the lids to show that they are empty.
2. Let the child see as you put the brick in one of the empty tins. Replace the lid and shake it so the child hears the noise it makes.
3. Encourage the child to shake the tin and make a noise.
4. Move the two tins around so that the child is not sure which one has the brick.
5. Shake one tin for several seconds and then shake the other tin for several seconds.
6. Ask the child which tin has the brick. (Avoid letting her shake the tin herself, as she may be able to guess from the weight of the tin.)
7. If the child seems unsure, shake the tin for a longer time. If she continues to have difficulty, shake the empty tin and open the lid, then shake the full one and open the lid.
8. Repeat steps 4–6.
9. Let the child open the tin when she has made the correct choice.

To increase the complexity of the activity
- shake the tin for a shorter period of time;
- use objects that make a quieter sound;
- increase the distance between you and the child.

Variations

- Vary pitch and volume by using different objects in the containers; for example, rice will have a different sound from pebbles.
- Vary pitch and volume by using different containers; for example, rice in a tin will have a different sound from rice in a plastic container.
- Put pictures on the front of the tins. The child has to name or sign the picture to indicate which container has the brick.
- Pretend to be a magician. Try wearing a top hat and waving a magic wand!

SOUND DETECTION: SOUND OR SILENCE
Activities for Early Years Settings

These activities will help the child to develop the ability to tell the difference between sound and silence. Choose one musical instrument or sound maker for each game, as the goal is to detect sound and not to recognize or distinguish between different sounds.

☐ *See the sound*

Let the child experience seeing sound as well as hearing it. Put some dried rice on the top of a drum, and watch the grains bounce around as you bang the drum. You can talk about how the rice moves when it makes a sound and stops when the drum is silent. An alternative is the ocean drum where you can see the balls inside moving as you hear the sound of the ocean.

☐ *Feel the sound*

Let the child experience feeling the vibrations a sound makes as well as hearing it. Some ideas are:

- standing barefoot next to a floor speaker playing a strong bass sound;
- touching a large cymbal struck with a mallet;
- holding a vibrator pad from an alarm clock for the deaf;
- feeling vibrations in the body from resonator tone bars (bass, contra bass and sub contra);

☐ *Sorting shakers*

You will need several shakers with different sounds and some empty or silent shakers. (You can make your own or use a commercial product.) Ask the child to sort them into groups of noisy shakers and silent shakers. The sounds do not have to be matched or the materials inside identified.

☐ *Find the noisy shaker*

Ask one child to close her eyes, while you give a noisy shaker to one child and a silent shaker to another. Ask her to open her eyes and listen to each shaker in turn. Can she guess who has the noisy shaker?

SOUND DETECTION: SOUND OR SILENCE
Activities for Home

These activities will help your child to develop the ability to tell the difference between sound and silence. Choose one musical instrument or sound maker for each game, as the goal is to detect sound and not to recognize or distinguish between different sounds.

☐ *Explore sound and silence*

Let your child explore the difference between 'sound' and its opposite 'silence'. Give her a noisy toy along with one that makes no sound: for example, a snow globe and a shaker or a squeaky doll with a soft teddy. Draw her attention to whether the toy has sound or is silent. At first, you may need to use gesture or sign to help her distinguish between the two.

☐ *Answer that please!*

Encourage your child to be aware of noises in the home, such as the doorbell or knocker or your phone ringing. Help her to pick up the phone or open the door. It does not matter if your child confuses the sounds at this stage. The aim is for her to show that she has heard a sound. You can take her to the correct sound.

☐ *Find the brick*

To play this game you will need two identical cardboard boxes with lids and one large wooden brick. Show your child the empty boxes. Shake each one and then remove the lids to show that they are empty. Let your child see as you put the brick in one of the empty boxes. Replace the lid and shake it so she hears the noise it makes. Encourage her to shake the box and make a noise.

Next, move the two boxes around so that the child is not sure which one has the brick. Can your child find the brick by listening to the boxes? Try this game using different containers and other toys or objects.

☐ *Full or empty*

Use some full and empty food boxes or jars for this activity. Choose foods that make a noise when the packet is shaken, such as cereals, tea or coffee in a jar. Can your child tell the difference between an empty packet and a full one? Let her shake the packet if she has difficulty with hearing the noise.

SOUND DETECTION: SOUND OR SILENCE
Musical Instruments and Sound Makers

Use a variety of musical instruments or sound makers. Choose instruments or sound makers where there is a clear difference between sound and no sound. For example, a drumbeat is a good sound maker for this activity. Mini sleigh bells are not, as they are very difficult to keep quiet.

Here are some ideas:

- ❏ drum (make your own by banging a stick on an upturned bucket)
- ❏ hand bell (hold the clapper inside to silence the bell)
- ❏ horn
- ❏ resonator tone bars
- ❏ recorded music
- ❏ music box
- ❏ musical toy
- ❏ doorbell
- ❏ door knocker
- ❏ alarm clock

The following items can be placed in shakers:

- ❏ toy plastic animals
- ❏ small toys
- ❏ beads
- ❏ rice
- ❏ pebbles or stones
- ❏ cotton reels

 Always be extremely careful with small objects, which may be swallowed accidentally by young children. Items should be placed in shakers with *secure* lids.

SOUND DETECTION: START AND FINISH
Teaching Activity

'Wakey Wakey'

You will need:
A puppet; a blanket; an alarm clock.

Useful words and phrases:
listen; look; "Wakey wakey"; blanket; sleeping.

What to do:

1. Tell the child that you are going to play a listening game with the alarm clock. Let her listen as you make the alarm go off. Draw her attention to the start and finish of the sound.

2. Next tell her the puppet (give it a name) is very sleepy. Lay him down under the blanket.

3. Tell the child to listen carefully. As soon as she hears the alarm clock she must help the puppet to wake up.

4. Once the alarm clock stops ringing, the naughty puppet wants to go back to sleep. Help the child put the puppet back under the blanket when the alarm finishes.

5. Repeat the activity several times, but allow the child to do the actions by herself.

To increase the complexity of the activity
- use a shorter alarm;
- increase the distance between the alarm clock and the child.

Variations
- Let the child have a turn at lying down under the blanket.
- Use other dolls or teddies.
- Use different sounds like a gong or music on a radio.

SOUND DETECTION: START AND FINISH
Activities for Early Years Settings

These activities will help develop the child's awareness of the start and end of sounds. Help the child by letting her watch as you make a sound or turn music on or off. Later, she can play the games by listening alone.

☐ *Everyday routines*

Draw the child's attention to the start and finish of noises in everyday routines.

☐ *Stop or start*

Use the start or the end of a sound to signal an activity: for example, the children have to wait until you finish ringing a bell before they line up for outside play.

☐ *Musical statues*

The children move around to the sound of a musical instrument or sound maker and freeze into a statue when it stops. Make the periods of silence between sounds longer and longer so it becomes more and more difficult for the children to stay still. Alternatively, quickly change from music to silence then back to music. Once they are familiar with both, alternate between long and short periods of silence or music.

☐ *Musical bumps*

This is a variation of musical statues but in this game, children sit down as soon as the music stops. Once the music starts again the children jump up and start over again. As in the musical statues game, alternate between long and short periods of silence or music.

☐ *Vice versa*

Try playing musical chairs and statues with the child moving around when there is no sound and stopping when the music is playing.

SOUND DETECTION: START AND FINISH
Activities for Home

These games will help develop your child's awareness of the start and finish of sounds. Help your child by letting her watch as you make a sound or turn the music on or off. Later, she can play the games by listening alone.

☐ *Music in the home*

Avoid having music playing continuously in the background. Have special times in the day when you listen to music with your child. Draw your child's attention to the start and the finish of musical sounds, such as the start of a song or the theme music of her favourite television programme signalling the end of the programme.

☐ *Music box*

You will need a wind-up music box. Encourage your child to make her doll or teddy dance to the music. When the music stops, the doll or teddy falls to the floor. Then the music starts again, and up dolly or teddy jump to dance again.

☐ *Musical chairs*

Your child and some family members or a group of children at a party can play musical chairs. They must move around to the sound of the music and then sit on a chair when the music stops. The catch is that a chair is taken away each time, and one person is out when she loses her seat. This is a good incentive to listen out for the finish of a sound.

SOUND DETECTION: START AND FINISH
Musical Instruments and Sound Makers

Choose musical instruments or sound makers where you have some control over making a clear start and finish to the sound. Avoid sounds that fade slowly, or ones that are too short and precise.

Here are some ideas:

- ❏ hand bell (hold the clapper inside to silence the bell)
- ❏ horn
- ❏ recorder
- ❏ flute
- ❏ recorded music
- ❏ music box
- ❏ musical toy
- ❏ alarm clock
- ❏ guiro
- ❏ maraca

The following items can be placed in shakers:

- ❏ toy plastic animals
- ❏ small toys
- ❏ beads
- ❏ rice
- ❏ pebbles or stones
- ❏ cotton reels

 Always be extremely careful with small objects, which may be swallowed accidentally by young children. Items should be placed in shakers with *secure* lids.

SOUND DETECTION: RESPONDING TO SOUND
Teaching Activity

'Beat that Drum'

You will need:
a drum with a loud and deep sound;
a beater;
a small screen;
stacking rings.

Useful words and phrases:
look; listen; drum;
sound/noise; loud; quiet;
ring; bang.

What to do:

1. Introduce the drum by showing it to the child and making some sounds. Let the child have a turn at playing it.

2. Play a beat on the drum and place a ring on the stick. (The sound and the placing of the ring should coincide so that the child associates the action with the drumbeat.)

3. Let the child have the next turn. Play another beat but this time help the child to place the ring on the stick.

4. Repeat this several times with the child watching and listening until she is consistently placing a ring on the stick.

5. Hide the drum behind the screen.

6. Give the child a ring to hold ready, and tell her to listen very hard for the noise of the drum. When she hears it, she must put the ring on the stick.

7. Avoid giving any unintentional clues when you make the drum beat, such as raised eyebrows, arm movements.

8. If the child has difficulty with the task, make several drum beats and increase the volume.

9. If she continues to have difficulty, let her watch again, until she is ready for an auditory task only.

Section 3: Sound Detection

To increase the complexity of the activity

- use fewer repetitions of the drumbeat;
- make the sound of the drum quieter.

Variations

- Let the child take a turn at making the sound for you to place the ring on the stick.
- Try using other simple construction toys, such as stacking beakers, brick towers and shape posting boxes.

SOUND DETECTION: RESPONDING TO SOUND
Activities for Early Years Settings

These games will help the child to *respond* to musical instruments and everyday sounds. Again choose one sound for each game, as the aim is to detect sound and not to recognize or distinguish between different sounds.

Action and movement games

Using one musical instrument or other sound maker, show the child how to make an action or movement when a sound is made. Actions could include clapping her hands or raising her arms in the air. Movements could include standing up and sitting down, taking a large stride, a hop or a skip. If two children play this game, one can make the sound while the other carries out an action or movement.

Home corner

Join the child in the home corner and play some sound games. The child could open a door to a loud knock. Make it fun by having different toys visiting – monkey gives a "hoot", the fairy does a dance, teddy wants a hug.

Stepping stones

Place stepping stones across the floor. When you make a sound like a beat on a drum or a hoot on a horn, the child can take one step. Play this with two children so one can make the sounds.

It's the postman!

Play this game with two or three children. One child brings the other children surprise presents. They must wait for the knock on the door or a ring on a buzzer before opening it for the postman. (The presents can be as simple as a picture cut from a magazine or a small toy.)

SOUND DETECTION: RESPONDING TO SOUND
Activities for Home

These games will help your child respond to sounds. At first, you may need to help your child by letting her see what is making the sound. Again choose one sound for each game, as the aim is to detect sound and not to recognize or distinguish between different sounds.

☐ *Jack in the box*

Let your child play the 'Jack' in 'Jack in the box'. You will need a large cardboard box. Your child hides in the box and waits for the signal. Make a loud sound by beating on a drum or banging a wooden spoon on an upturned biscuit tin. Encourage your child to pop out when she hears the sound. The top of the box can have a loose-fitting lid, attached on one side, to make it more fun for her to 'pop' out.

☐ *Knock knock*

Play this game with your child and one other adult. One adult leaves the room, while the other adult encourages the child to listen for a knock or the ring of a bell. Your child must open the door when she hears you make a nice loud knock. Give her a surprise present each time, such as a paper hat, a small toy or let her blow some bubbles. She only gets a present if she waits for you to knock. Try to make the time she has to wait longer and longer.

☐ *Toy telephone*

Record the sound of your phone ringing so you can play a 'pretend' game with your child. When your child hears the ring, she must pick up her toy telephone.

SOUND DETECTION: RESPONDING TO SOUND
Sounds and Sound Makers

Choose sounds or sound makers where there is a clear difference between sound and no sound. Use the musical instruments listed in previous sections. These can be combined with everyday sounds. (It may be easier to record these sounds on your phone or tablet to play to the child.)

Here are some ideas for everyday sounds:

- ☐ alarm clock
- ☐ phone
- ☐ music box
- ☐ door knocker
- ☐ doorbell/buzzer
- ☐ television
- ☐ musical instrument

SOUND DETECTION: SYMBOLIC SOUNDS
Teaching Activity

'Farmyard'

You will need:
a farmyard model;
several plastic shapes of cows; a box.

Useful words and phrases:
look; listen; cow;
"moo"; farm;
sound or noise.

What to do:

1. Set up the farmyard model on a table. Show the child the toy cows and allow her to play with them for a few minutes.

2. Explain that you are going to play a listening game. Place the cows in a box and put this to one side.

3. Give the child one of the toy cows, and tell her to listen carefully. Make a mooing sound and prompt her to place the toy cow in the farmyard.

4. Repeat the game with another toy cow. This time see if the child can place the cow in the farmyard without any prompts.

5. Next cover your mouth with your hand when you make the sound, so that the child has to rely on listening alone.

6. If the child has difficulty, repeat the sound and then prompt her to place the cow in the farmyard.

7. Continue the game until all the cows are placed in the farmyard.

Section 3: Sound Detection

To increase the complexity of the activity

- use fewer repetitions of the animal sounds;
- make shorter animal sounds;
- make quieter animal sounds.

Variations

- Introduce other animal sounds, but remember to only use one animal sound at a time.
- Play this game with a group of children. The sounds will be repeated many times, increasing the listening practice for the child. An older child can be included in the group to model the appropriate responses for the other children.
- Play recorded sounds.
- Make a paper pathway for the model farm that leads from the field to the barn. The child has to move the animal along the pathway one square at a time when she hears the noise.

SOUND DETECTION: SYMBOLIC SOUNDS
Activities for Early Years Settings

These activities will help the child to listen and respond to symbolic sounds that represent things like objects, animals, feelings and actions. Remember to use only one sound at a time, otherwise the child will need to know the sound in order to produce the appropriate action.

☐ *Animals on the farm*

Set out a model farm or use a farm layout. Choose one animal and a suitable sound, for example, a "quack" for a duck. Show the child how to place the duck in the pond when you say a sound. Play this game with other animals – a "moo" for a cow to go in a shed; or a "baaaah" for a sheep to go in a field.

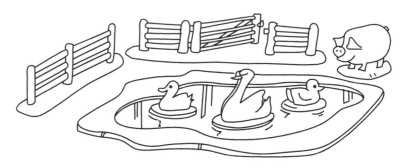

☐ *Fun at the park*

Use small doll material with a slide or roundabout to play this game. Choose one sound and action to play with the child. This could be the sound "weee" with dolly going down the slide. Make the sound and encourage the child to carry out the action. Other actions might be taking a spin on the roundabout or going on a swing.

☐ *Puppets*

Use a puppet that the child has to wake up when the alarm clock starts ringing. You and the child could also take turns at pretending to be asleep and waking up to the alarm. Make a big yawn and stretch up your arms.

☐ *Posting box*

Gather together several pictures of the same animal. Each child must wait for you to make the sound of the animal first before posting a picture in the box.

☐ *Jumping frogs*

Collect together some toy frogs or make some out of cardboard. Make one of the frogs jump in a bucket when you make a croaking sound. Encourage the child to wait for the sound before she helps the frog jump. (Add water and some leaves to make it like a real pond!)

SOUND DETECTION: SYMBOLIC SOUNDS
Activities for Home

These activities will help your child to listen and respond to symbolic sounds that represent things like objects, animals, feelings and actions. Concentrate on one sound at a time, and do lots of repetition. If your child copies a sound, copy her back and carry out an action in response.

☐ *Park the car*

You will need a toy car and a garage. (An old shoebox can be turned upside down and a hole put in one side to make a 'pretend' garage.) Give your child the car and make a sound like a car engine – "vroom". Help your child to push the car into the garage. Next time, see if she can wait for the sound before she parks the car.

☐ *Animal sounds*

Play a game with animal puppets or soft toys. A cat can be stroked when you say "miaow". A dog can jump up and down when you say "Woof-woof."

☐ *In the dog house*

Use a soft toy and an old box for a kennel. Give your child the toy dog and say "Woof-woof". Help your child to put the dog in its kennel. Next time, see if she can wait for the sound before she puts the dog inside.

☐ *On the slide*

Take your child on the slide at the park. She must wait for you to call out "weee" before she slides down. At home she can play the same game with her dolls or teddies. Use a shiny book or piece of wood for the slide.

SOUND DETECTION
Symbolic Sounds

Here are some suggestions for symbolic sounds. Remember some children and families may use different sounds, so adapt the activity to incorporate these more familiar sounds for the child.

- ❏ "weee" – push dolly down the slide
- ❏ "weee" – dolly has a spin on a roundabout
- ❏ "beep beep" – drive a car along a road
- ❏ "ding ding" – ring the bell on the bus
- ❏ "vroom" – drive a bus or car into a garage
- ❏ "choo choo" – push the train through the tunnel
- ❏ "chchch choo" – train rushing along the track
- ❏ "tick tock" – turn the clock on its face
- ❏ "tweet tweet" – pop a toy bird in a cage
- ❏ animal sounds (see list in 'Sounds, Sound Makers and Musical Instruments').

SOUND DETECTION
Record Sheet

Child's name	

Date	Activity/Context	Observations
Example 21.9.	*Playing 'musical bumps' with a small group of children. Teaching assistant using recorded music.*	*Lots of giggling and excitement. Skipping and dancing around the room. Sitting down with other children. Watching for sound being switched on or off.*

AI = adult initiated activity; CI = child initiated activity

SECTION 4
Sound Recognition

Introduction 49

Same/Different 50

    Teaching Activity 50

    Activities for Early Years Settings 52

    Activities for Home 54

    Sounds and Sound makers 55

Musical Instruments 56

    Teaching Activity 56

    Activities for Early Years Settings 58

    Activities for Home 59

    Musical Instruments 60

Everyday Sounds 61

    Teaching Activity 61

    Activities for Early Years Settings 63

Activities for Home *64*

Sounds and Sound Makers *66*

Animal Sounds *67*

Teaching Activity *67*

Activities for Early Years Settings *69*

Activities for Home *71*

Sounds and Sound Makers *73*

Record Sheet *74*

INTRODUCTION

The activities in this section are designed to develop the child's ability to recognize sound and give meaning to it. Children should be able to detect sound and make simple discriminations (same/different) before attempting sound recognition activities. At this stage, the child is able to identify sounds without necessarily having the ability to name the sound or the source of the sound. They may use sound rather than words to represent objects and events, such as "quack quack" for duck and "weee" for going down a slide.

Children will begin to attach meaning to sound by associating what they hear with the source of the sound. The ability to identify sound is essential to the development of the child's listening and language skills, which children with a hearing loss often need to improve.

The activities require a range of responses, including matching sound makers, responding to a sound signal and identifying recorded sounds. They are therefore suitable for children with limited vocabulary like EAL learners. These games are also useful for improving concentration and memory.

SOUND RECOGNITION: SAME/DIFFERENT
Teaching Activity

'Spot the Difference'

You will need:
two identical shakers;
one drum; a screen.

Useful words and phrases:
look; listen; same-different; shaker(s);
drum; first; last-second; sound.

What to do:

1. Introduce the shakers to the child. Talk about how they look and sound the same. Let the child have a turn at playing with them and comparing the sounds.

2. Put the shakers to one side when the child has finished playing and introduce the drum. Let the child have a turn at banging it.

3. Next choose one shaker and make a sound, then beat the drum. Point out to the child how the sound is different.

4. Explain to the child that you are going to play a listening game. Place one of the shakers in front of the child but out of reach. Place the other shaker and drum behind the screen.

5. Make sure the child is ready and then tell her to listen carefully. Make a sound with the shaker in sight and then a second sound behind the screen using either the other shaker or the drum. (Some children may need to hear the shaker two or three times *before* a sound is made by the instrument behind the screen.)

6. Ask the child if the sounds are the same or different.

7. Let the child see the second sound maker when she has chosen. If she has made a mistake, play the sounds again.

8. Repeat until the child has had several turns.

Section 4: Sound Recognition

To increase the complexity of the activity

- introduce instruments that sound increasingly similar;
- introduce a delay before making the second sound.

Variations

- Vary the musical instruments.
- Let the child make the sounds.

SOUND RECOGNITION: SAME/DIFFERENT
Activities for Early Years Settings

These activities are designed to develop the child's ability to make simple discriminations between sounds by deciding whether two sounds are the same or different. This is the first step towards the ability to discriminate one sound from another.

Find the odd one out

You will need several matching shakers. Choose two matching shakers (AA). Place one A with two other, non-matching shakers (BB). (See illustration.) Mix up the shakers. Give the child the remaining A shaker. Can she find its matching shaker amongst the three? Put identifying marks on the bottom of the containers so that the child is able to check if she is correct.

Find the matching instrument – barrier game

You will need pairs of matching instruments to play this game. Let the child explore the instruments. Talk about how the sounds are the same. Hide one set of instruments behind a screen, and place the matching instruments on the table in front of the child. The child chooses an instrument from the table. She must listen while you play an instrument behind the screen. Can she tell if the sounds are the same? Two children can play this as a barrier game. If they get it right, they get a counter. At the end, the winner is the one with the most counters.

Team games

Divide the children into two teams, and provide them with pairs of matching shakers divided equally between the two groups. Can each child

Section 4: Sound Recognition

pair up with the other child who has the same sound? When the children have found a partner, they sit together on the floor. Try giving the children a time limit.

☐ *Odd one out*

Record two sounds from musical instruments. (Choose ones that are very dissimilar). Play the sounds to the child. Ask her to put up her hand when the sound is different. Always keep the first sound the same; that is, A A or A B. Gradually introduce more sounds - A A A or A A B.

☐ *Sound Pelmanism*

Play sound Pelmanism with several different pairs of matching shakers. Mix up the shakers, and place them on the table. Take turns with the child to select two shakers. The winner is the one who finds the most matching pairs. You might want to use shakers that have a lid that can easily be removed to check the sound maker, for example, a screw top lid or plastic snap lid.

SOUND RECOGNITION: SAME/DIFFERENT
Activities for Home

These games will help your child to learn about the way sounds can be the same or different. This can be a good first activity before you start with more difficult sound recognition games.

☐ *Sounds the same*

Draw your child's attention to the way two objects make the same sound. Make one sound, followed by a matching sound. Try some of the following:

- dropping two cotton reels
- shaking two boxes of paper clips
- shaking two bunches of keys
- shaking pegs in tins

☐ *Copy a sound*

If your child makes a sound with an object, try to make the same sound. If your child drops a brick, show her how you can make the same sound by dropping another brick.

☐ *Gift boxes*

Wrap up some sound makers in identical gift boxes. The child has to find the two that match and open them. You can use small toys and bricks that will rattle about and will also give your child something to play with when the box is opened. Use some 'Tin Animal Sound Makers', which will make an animal sound when turned over.

SOUND RECOGNITION: SAME/DIFFERENT
Sound Makers

You may carry out same/different activities with a wide variety of musical instruments or sound makers. Choose ones that sound dissimilar. So sleigh bells and a tambourine are not a good match. Sleigh bells with a drum would be ideal.

Here are some ideas:
Musical instruments

- ☐ maraca
- ☐ drum
- ☐ rhythm sticks
- ☐ jingle bells
- ☐ guiro

- ☐ triangles
- ☐ tambourines
- ☐ glockenspiel
- ☐ mouth organ
- ☐ recorder

The following items can be placed in shakers:

- ☐ toy plastic animals
- ☐ small toys
- ☐ model vehicles
- ☐ keys

- ☐ beads
- ☐ pegs
- ☐ pebbles or stones
- ☐ cotton reels

 Always be extremely careful with small objects, which may be swallowed accidentally by young children. Items should be placed in shakers with *secure* lids. If in any doubt, use larger objects or toys.

SOUND RECOGNITION: MUSICAL INSTRUMENTS
Teaching Activity

'Action to sound'

You will need:
a drum; a hand bell.

Useful words and phrases:
look; listen; clap (hands);
stamp feet; wait; drum; bells.

What to do:

1. Demonstrate the sound that the drum makes. Let the child have a turn at playing the drum.

2. Explain that you want her to stamp her feet when she hears the drum beat. Play the drum and encourage her to stamp her feet.

3. When she is confident with this task, introduce the bell and demonstrate the sound it makes.

4. Let the child have a turn at playing the bell. (For some children with poor attention skills, it would be better to put the first instrument away before showing the other one.)

5. Explain to the child that you want her to clap her hands when she hears the bell. Shake the bell and encourage her to clap her hands.

6. When she is confident with this task, repeat the activity, using both instruments. Make a sound with the drum. Does she remember to stamp her feet? Make a sound with the bell. Does she remember to clap her hands?

7. When the child is responding appropriately with the instruments in sight, hide the drum and bell behind a screen.

8. Ask her to listen carefully.

9. Choose an instrument and make a sound. If she makes a mistake, repeat the sound. If she continues to have difficulty, show her the instrument and encourage her to make the appropriate action. Now try with the instrument hidden again.

10. Continue with the activity until the child is confidently matching action to sound.

Section 4: Sound Recognition

To increase the complexity of the activity

- introduce musical instruments that sound increasingly similar;
- ask the child to respond to a sequence of musical instruments (three maximum);
- use less familiar sounds;
- introduce a delay before the child is allowed to respond.

Variations

- Introduce different actions such as waving hands, rubbing tummy, lifting arms up or touching the floor.
- Let the child have a turn at making the sounds. You carry out the appropriate action.

SOUND RECOGNITION: MUSICAL INSTRUMENTS
Activities for Early Years Settings

These activities will help the child to recognize and respond to different musical instruments. At first, let the child watch as you make the sound with the instruments. Later, you can hide the instruments so the child is relying on her listening skills alone.

☐ Action and movement games

Play this game with one child or a group of children. Teach the child to perform an action or movement to the sound of a musical instrument. Start with one instrument and one action or movement. Actions could include clapping hands, standing up or waving arms in the air. Movements could include walking very fast, hopping, taking large strides, skipping or dancing. Once the child is confident with one instrument, you can introduce another one with a different action. Play the instruments out of sight. Can the children carry out the right action?

☐ Matching the instrument to a picture

Place two or three pictures of different musical instruments around the room. Use instruments that match the pictures to make some sounds out of sight. Can the child find the matching picture?

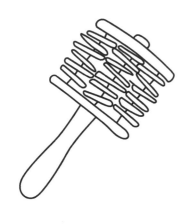

☐ Giant picture lotto

Make a giant picture lotto. Pictures of musical instruments are drawn in the different squares on the lotto. Use real instruments to make some sounds. When the child hears a sound, she has to place a matching picture on the correct square. At the end she can choose to hear different instruments by selecting pictures from the lotto.

☐ Team games

Divide the children into two teams. Each team must listen for a sound from a musical instrument. For example, team A listens for a drum and team B listens for a tambourine. When they hear the sound of their musical instrument, the team can move across the room. When the sound stops, they must stand still. Make the sounds out of sight, alternating the instruments. The winner is the team that gets across the room first. (Give the teams different movements to carry out, such as skipping, hopping or walking backwards.)

☐ Everyday routines

Use different sounds to signal different activities: for example, a bell for lunch, a whistle for the end of outside play.

SOUND RECOGNITION: MUSICAL INSTRUMENTS
Activities for Home

Your child will learn to recognize musical instruments by listening to and copying sounds. At first, let your child watch as you make the sound with the objects. Later, you can hide the objects behind the sofa or a large piece of card, so your child is relying on her listening skills alone.

☐ *Match a sound*

You will need two matching musical instruments or musical toys like an egg shaker or squeaker. (Homemade instruments can be used.) Make sure you and your child have one set of instruments each. Show the child how you can make a sound with your instrument. Encourage her to copy you with her matching instrument. Later, you can hide your instrument. Can she copy the sound by listening alone? When she is familiar with the game, introduce another instrument.

☐ *Dancing*

Have some sounds of musical instruments recorded on your phone or tablet. Teach your child to do simple dances to different musical sounds. She could march to the beat of a drum or tiptoe to the sound of wind chimes. See if she can remember the dances if you play the instruments out of sight.

☐ *Instruments around the world*

Not many musical instruments at home? Then watch and listen to the video 'Sesame Street Music Maker : Worldly Instruments'.
https://www.youtube.com/watch?time_continue=130&v=oT0vLdiZQzo

Listen to some great instruments from around the world. (Tip: You can skip the descriptions and go straight to the sounds by clicking on instruments.)

SOUND RECOGNITION: MUSICAL INSTRUMENTS
Musical Instruments

You may carry out sound recognition activities with a variety of musical instruments or music makers, such as the following:

- ❏ maraca
- ❏ drum
- ❏ shaker
- ❏ rhythm sticks
- ❏ jingle bells
- ❏ triangles
- ❏ tambourines
- ❏ glockenspiel
- ❏ mouth organ
- ❏ recorder

Homemade musical instruments

- ❏ wind chimes
- ❏ musical mobile
- ❏ empty tin and a wooden spoon (drum)
- ❏ frying pan or saucepan lid (gong)
- ❏ rattle
- ❏ two sticks to tap together

SOUND RECOGNITION: EVERYDAY SOUNDS
Teaching Activity

'Guess the Object'

You will need:
two identical sets of sound making everyday objects – two bunches of keys; two spoons; two cups (stir spoon in cup to make a sound); a screen.

Useful words and phrases:
listen; look; sound; wait; point; name of objects; hide.

What to do:

1. This activity can be carried out at a table or on the floor.

2. Introduce each object to the child by naming it and making a sound. Allow the child a few moments to explore the object. (For some children with poor attention skills it would be better to put one object away before showing another one.)

3. Place one set of the everyday objects in front of the child. They should be within easy reach of the child, but not so close that they are tempted to immediately pick them up.

4. Show the child that you have matching objects. Place your duplicate set near to you but still in sight of the child.

5. Ask the child to look and listen. Choose one object from your duplicate set and make a sound in her sight. Ask the child to find the matching object from her set.

6. If she is unsure or makes an incorrect choice, hold your object close to the duplicate one in her set. Give her your object to make a sound. Then repeat the task with the same object.

7. Continue until the child is consistently matching the objects by watching and listening.

8. Hide your objects behind a screen. Make a sound for several seconds and ask the child to find the matching object from her duplicate set.

Copyright material from Diana Williams (2020), *Early Listening Skills for Children with a Hearing Loss*, Second Edition, Routledge

Section 4: Sound Recognition

9 If the child is unsuccessful on the first attempt, repeat the sound exactly. If she is still unsure or chooses incorrectly, make the sound in her sight.

10 Allow the child to play briefly with the object when she has made the correct choice.

To increase the complexity of the activity

- introduce objects that sound increasingly similar;
- ask the child to identify more than one object at a time (three maximum);
- use less familiar objects;
- introduce a delay before the child is allowed to respond.

Variations

- Vary the objects.
- In a group game, the children can take turns to make the sounds for the other children.

SOUND RECOGNITION: EVERYDAY SOUNDS
Activities for Early Years Settings

These activities help the child to recognize sounds made by everyday objects. At first, let the child see you make the sounds. Later, you can hide the sound maker so the child is relying on her listening skills alone.

☐ Match my object

You will need some everyday objects. These could be buttons in a box or a spoon in a cup. Make sure that you and the child have one each of the everyday objects. Show the child how you can make a sound with one of the objects. Encourage her to copy you. At first, she may need to make sounds along with you. Later, you can hide the objects. Can she copy the sounds by listening alone? Try this game using a variety of everyday objects.

☐ Matching object to sound

Use two or three everyday objects, which have matching pictures (use large flashcards). Make a sound with one of the objects. Can the child point to the appropriate picture? Hide the objects behind a screen. Can she find the correct picture by listening to the sound alone?

☐ Giant picture lotto

Make a giant picture lotto. Draw pictures of different sound making objects in the different squares on the lotto. Use real everyday objects to make the sounds. When the child hears a sound, she has to place a matching picture on the correct square. At the end, the children can choose to hear different sounds by selecting object pictures from the lotto.

☐ Sound shakers

Place small objects like cotton reels or buttons in opaque shakers. Let the child see the objects being placed in the shakers and then listen to the sound they make. Mix up the containers. Make a sound with one of the shakers. Can the child identify the object from the sound? Have some duplicate objects in a transparent container for the child to indicate which objects made the sound if they are unsure of the object names.

SOUND RECOGNITION: EVERYDAY SOUNDS
Activities for Home

These activities will help your child to recognize the sound made by everyday objects. Do not worry at this stage about your child naming the objects. At first, let your child watch as you make the sound with the objects. Later, you can hide the objects behind the sofa or a large piece of card, so your child is relying on her listening skills alone.

☐ *Walk round the home*

Ask your child to listen for a particular sound or sounds as you walk round your home. Your child could listen for the ticking of the alarm clock in the bedroom, the whirr of the fridge in the kitchen and the post coming through the door in the hall. Talk about the sounds you hear.

☐ *What made that sound?*

Draw your child's attention to sounds like the doorbell or the phone. Encourage her to help you answer the door or pick up the phone. If she confuses two sounds, show her what is making the sound. Repeat the sound for her if you can, for example, by ringing the doorbell again.

☐ *Tap an object*

Tap an object in the room. Use a wooden spoon or stick. (Be careful – do not hit your best china!) Can your child tap the same object? Ask her to close her eyes while you go around the room tapping objects. Can she still tap the same objects as you just by hearing the sound?

☐ *Record a sound*

Record your child making different sounds around the house (see the previous activity). Take photos and record the sound on a phone or tablet. You can play the sounds on another day. Can your child recognize the sound and find the object? Show her the photo if she is unsure.

Section 4: Sound Recognition

☐ *Surprise box*

Make a 'surprise box' by placing objects in a box. Make a sound with one of the everyday objects. Keep it out of sight by holding it inside the box. Stop making the sound – can your child find the object?

☐ *Mime*

Show the child how to mime using different sound making objects in the home. Each time she hears the sound she must mime using the object; for example, phone – mime holding the phone; vacuum cleaner – mime vacuuming the carpet.

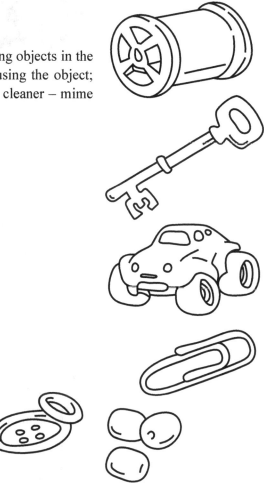

SOUND RECOGNITION: EVERYDAY SOUNDS
Sounds and Sound Makers

You may carry out sound recognition activities with a variety of everyday objects such as the following:

- ☐ keys
- ☐ spoon in a cup or glass
- ☐ book shutting or dropping
- ☐ crunchy paper
- ☐ water being poured
- ☐ knife scraping on a plate
- ☐ pencil scribbling
- ☐ fingers tapping on a table or window
- ☐ stamping feet
- ☐ phone
- ☐ alarm clock
- ☐ radio
- ☐ music box
- ☐ door knocker or bell
- ☐ vacuum cleaner
- ☐ washing machine
- ☐ toilet flushing
- ☐ cooking sounds
- ☐ footsteps
- ☐ pet noises (barking, miaowing)
- ☐ doors banging
- ☐ cleaning sounds (sweeping, rubbing)

The following items can be placed in shakers:

- ☐ toy plastic animals
- ☐ small toys
- ☐ model vehicles
- ☐ keys
- ☐ beads
- ☐ pegs
- ☐ pebbles or stones
- ☐ cotton reels

 Always be extremely careful with small objects, which may be swallowed accidentally by young children. Items should be placed in shakers with *secure* lids. If in any doubt, use larger objects or toys.

SOUND RECOGNITION: ANIMAL SOUNDS
Teaching Activity

'Animal Puppets'

You will need:
two pairs of animal puppets (for example, a cat and a dog); a large opaque bag.

Useful words and phrases:
listen; look; animal names; animal noises; bag.

What to do:

1. Introduce one set of puppets to the child. Allow the child to try on each puppet and to play with it for a few minutes.

2. Name the animals and ask the child about her own pets. Make the sounds for each of the puppets.

3. Tell the child you have some more animals hidden in the bag. She must listen carefully for the sound of the animal.

4. Put your hand in the bag and put on one of the puppets. Make the appropriate noise for several seconds.

5. Ask the child to show you which animal is making the noise.

6. If the child fails to make the correct response, repeat the sound. It may be necessary to cue the child by pointing to the puppet on the table or imitating some of the characteristics of the animal; for example, a cat may lick her paw. Select the animal puppet for the child if this fails to elicit the correct response.

7. During the activity, it is acceptable for the child to join in with making the sounds or naming the animals. This can be reinforced by the adult by copying the child. However, responses should not be forced from the child.

8. When the animal has been correctly identified, bring out the matching puppet from the bag and make the noise again.

9. Let the child try on the puppet and make the noise. This will reward and reinforce the child's learning.

To increase the complexity of the activity

- gradually increase the number of animal sounds (three maximum);
- introduce animal noises that sound increasingly similar;
- use less familiar animal sounds;
- introduce a delay before the child responds.

Variations

- Vary the animals and animal sounds.
- Use miniature toys instead of puppets.
- Record some animal sounds.
- Let the child have a turn at making the noises.

SOUND RECOGNITION: ANIMAL SOUNDS
Activities for Early Years Settings

These activities will help the child to recognize different animal sounds. At first, let the children watch your face as you make the animal sound. Later, you can hide your face with a large card or use recorded sounds so that the children are relying on their listening skills alone.

☐ *Lost animals*

You will need several animal puppets. Explain to the children that they are going to be zoo keepers and that several animals have escaped. Their job is to round up the lost animals and collect them in the bag for return to the zoo. Hide several animal puppets around the room, and tell the children to listen very carefully. When the children hear a sound they must find the animal that is making the noise. (Make the sounds near to the children, and not the animal puppets. Otherwise, the children will have to locate the sound as well as identify it.) If the children are incorrect, the animal is released again. (You could also try lost animals with a farmer or a pet shop owner.)

☐ *Find the matching picture*

You will need several animal pictures with matching miniature animals. Place the pictures on a table with the miniatures to one side. Ask the child to place the miniature animal on the matching picture when she hears the appropriate sound. (Sounds can be made by the adult or recorded.)

☐ *Sound lotto*

Sounds from animals are recorded. Pictures of the animals are presented in the form of a lotto card. The child has to place a counter on the picture that matches the appropriate sound.

Section 4: Sound Recognition

☐ *Giant picture lotto*

Make a giant picture lotto. Draw pictures of animals in the different squares on the lotto. Use recorded animal sounds. When the child hears a sound, she has to place a matching picture on the correct square. At the end the child can choose to hear different animal sounds by selecting pictures from the lotto.

☐ *Animal silhouettes*

Use several plastic animal shapes. Ask the child to draw around the shape when she hears the animal sound. She can colour in the picture to make the animal silhouettes.

SOUND RECOGNITION: ANIMAL SOUNDS
Activities for Home

Your child will learn to recognize animal sounds by listening to and copying sounds. At first, let your child watch your face as you make the animal sound. Later, you can cover your mouth with your hand so that your child is just listening.

❏ *'Old MacDonald had a Farm'*

Sing this song. Encourage your child to join in with the animal sounds. Show your child pictures of the animals when you make the sounds. Can your child point to the appropriate picture when you make the sound?

❏ *'Baa Baa Black Sheep'*

Teach your child this rhyme. Encourage her to join in with the sheep sounds. Do you know any other rhymes with animal sounds?

❏ *Animal stories*

Look at animal picture books. Make a sound and ask your child to find the animal. She can make sounds for you to find the picture.

❏ *Mime this animal*

Talk about animals your child has seen in books or at the zoo. Make the animal noises while you mime appropriate actions. You could:

- ❏ miaow and pretend to lick a paw;
- ❏ bark and pant like a dog;
- ❏ roar and make your hands like the claws of a tiger;
- ❏ say, "quack quack" and make your hand like a beak;
- ❏ moo and pretend to chew grass.

Make a sound. Can your child mime the animal?

❏ *Record your pet*

Do you have lots of pets? Then play this game. Help your child to record the sounds of her pets on your phone or tablet. Have some pet pictures ready. Play the sound of one of her pets. Can she find the right picture?

Copyright material from Diana Williams (2020), *Early Listening Skills for Children with a Hearing Loss*, Second Edition, Routledge

Section 4: Sound Recognition

☐ *Animal masks*

Help your child to make large colourful animal masks out of card and string. Make sure the mask has holes for the eyes and nose. Encourage your child to make animal sounds. Wear a mask yourself and make some sounds.

☐ *I am a . . .*

Paint an animal face on your child. (Special face paints can be bought from toy shops.) Encourage your child to make the sound of the animal.

SOUND RECOGNITION: ANIMAL SOUNDS
Sounds and Sound Makers

Animals can be represented by a variety of toys and other items:

- ❏ cuddly animal toys
- ❏ plastic animal shapes
- ❏ pictures or photographs of animals
- ❏ miniature animals
- ❏ animal masks

The following is a list of animal sounds that can be used in sound recognition games:

- ❏ cat – miaow
- ❏ dog – woof woof
- ❏ cow – moo
- ❏ pig – oink
- ❏ duck – quack
- ❏ horse – neigh
- ❏ sheep – baa
- ❏ chicken – cluck
- ❏ cockerel – cock-a-doodle-doo
- ❏ bear – growl
- ❏ monkey – oo-oo
- ❏ lion – roar
- ❏ bee – buzz
- ❏ bird – whistle or cheep

SOUND RECOGNITION
Record Sheet

Child's name	

Date	Activity/Context	Observations
Example 23.2.	*'Same/Different' Playing odd one out with three matching shakers. (AI)*	*Able to spot the odd sound from a choice of two. With prompts and repetition, able to find the odd one out in a choice of three shakers. Liked making a sound with the shakers.*

AI = adult initiated activity; CI = child initiated activity

SECTION 5
Finding Sound

Introduction 77

    Guidelines for Finding Sound 78

    Hints for Parents 80

Musical Instruments 81

    Teaching Activity 81

    Activities for Early Years Settings 83

    Activities for Home 85

    Sound Makers and Musical Instruments 86

Animal Sounds 87

    Teaching Activity 87

    Activities for Early Years Settings 89

    Activities for Home 91

    Animal Sound Makers 92

Action Sounds *93*

    Teaching Activity *93*

    Activities for Early Years Settings................................ *95*

    Activities for Home.. *96*

    Action Sounds.. *97*

Environmental Sounds *98*

    Teaching Activity *98*

    Activities for Early Years Settings............................... *100*

    Activities for Home.. *102*

    Environmental Sounds.. *103*

Record Sheet.. *104*

INTRODUCTION

This *section* contains activities designed to help develop the child's ability to localize or perceive the direction of a sound source in the space or environment around her. This is an important auditory skill for communication and for safety reasons. The ability to localize sound will help the child identify speakers, enabling her to respond appropriately to others and engage in conversations. Sound location is also vital for basic safety reasons: for example, when we cross the road, we are partly looking for cars and partly listening. A car approaching us from behind will be heard before it is seen.

We need to hear sound in both ears to localize a sound, so it is not surprising that some children with a hearing loss have difficulties with recognizing the direction of a sound source. Children with a unilateral or one-sided deafness, who hear in one ear only, are at a particular disadvantage.

It is essential for sound localization that the child is able to hear equally loud on both sides. Hearing technologies might help achieve this for the child. Seek the advice of a teacher of the deaf, educational audiologist or specialist speech and language therapist about the suitability of sound location activities. For some children it may be more appropriate to use communication strategies and classroom technology to counter difficulties with sound location.

The following activities are for those children who are likely to benefit from specific experience and listening practice in localizing sounds. It is important that sounds are presented at the appropriate distance, height and angle to the child as she develops this skill. The guidelines in this section give advice on how to present sounds to the child. This is based on the developmental stages of sound location in the young infant and the auditory needs of children with a hearing loss.

It is particularly important in sound localization that parents are given careful advice on how to carry out the activities. Use the 'Hints for Parents' sheet (p. 80) to record information for the parent.

FINDING SOUND
Guidelines for Finding Sound

The sound source should be at a distance from the child of one metre or less when she is beginning to learn sound localization. This distance can be increased as the child's skills develop. The position of the sound maker is also important. The child will respond first to sounds made at the side and level with the ear.

Decide at what height and angle you will present the sounds to the child. Use the hierarchy below, which is based on the developmental stages of sound location in the young infant.

  at the side and level with the right ear;

at the side and level with the left ear;

 at the side and level with the ear on either side;

at the side and below the right ear;

at the side and below the left ear;

at the side and above the right ear;

Section 5: Finding Sound

at the side and above the left ear;

at any angle to the ear (that is behind, to the side or in front of the ear).

Remember that some children may be responding to other cues in localization activities – they may see your shadow or smell your scent rather than hear the bell you are ringing!

FINDING SOUND
Hints for Parents

Ask your teacher of the deaf, educational audiologist or specialist speech and language therapist about the following:

- how far from your child to make the sound;
- where to hold the sound maker: for example, next to her ear, behind her;
- how loud to make the sound.

Make the sounds for your child:

- ☐ at the same height as your child's ear
- ☐ at the side of your child
- ☐ behind your child
- ☐ above your child's ear
- ☐ below your child's ear
- ☐ at. . . . . distance

Remember that your child may be using other cues to find the sound. She may see your shadow or smell your scent.

FINDING SOUND: MUSICAL INSTRUMENTS
Teaching Activity

'Point to the Sound'

You will need:
two identical shakers; three chairs of the same height.

Useful words and phrases:
listen; look; close your eyes; where is the sound?; who made the sound?; right; left; middle; point; make a noise.

What to do:

This activity is designed for three children but it can be played with one child and two adults. Place three chairs in a row so that the two outer chairs face the middle one at right angles (see illustration). There should be approximately one metre of space between each chair. Make sure that the seating arrangement allows sounds to be presented at ear level.

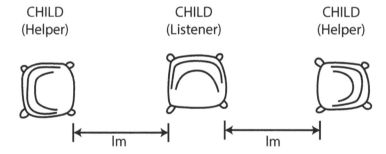

1. Sit one child in the middle. Two other children should take up positions as helpers at the side of her.

2. Give each helper at the side a shaker to hold.

3. Explain to the child in the middle that a sound will be made, which might come from her right side or her left. (Or use the names of the children if this is easier for the child.)

4. Indicate to one of the helpers at the side that they should make a noise with the shaker. (Use pointing or some other agreed signal.)

5. Ask the child in the middle to point to the one who made the sound.

6. Once the child is familiar with the task and is consistently pointing to the sound, ask her to close her eyes and then repeat the activity. A blindfold can be used if she is agreeable.

Section 5: Finding Sound

7 If the child makes a mistake, ask her to look while the sound is repeated.

8 When the child is correct, give positive feedback, so that she is clear about her success. Again allow her to see who has made the sound.

To increase the complexity of the activity

- make the sound of the shaker quieter;
- gradually increase the distance between the child and the shaker;
- use fewer repetitions of the sound;
- gradually change the angle of the shaker to the child (see guidelines on pp. 78–79).

Variations

- Give each child at the side an empty shoebox, which has one side cut out so the shaker can be hidden away. (Egg shakers would be an ideal instrument.) This way, the middle child can keep her eyes open.
- Vary the musical instruments used.

FINDING SOUND: MUSICAL INSTRUMENTS
Activities for Early Years Settings

These activities will help the child in locating sound. Games using musical instruments are more fun for the child, and many do not require her to understand or use language.

☐ *Find the musical instrument*

Sit one child in the middle of a small circle of children and give her a picture of a musical instrument. She closes her eyes or is blindfolded while the children pass the instrument around the group. At a signal from you, the children stop and the child holding the instrument uses it to make a noise and then hides it. The listener in the middle must give the picture to the child she thinks has made the noise. (Make sure the children are well spaced out for this activity.)

☐ *Who has the bell?*

Sit one child in the middle of a small circle of children. She closes her eyes while you give one child a bell, small enough to hide in her hand. Tell the children in the circle to shake their clenched hands in the air. The child in the middle is asked to open her eyes and point to the one who has the bell. (Make sure the children are well spaced out for this activity.)

 Use large or jumbo-sized sleigh or liberty bells, as smaller bells present a choking hazard. Supervise and store bell carefully.

☐ *Sound in stories*

Select a story that provides plenty of opportunity for using a musical instrument to represent a word or sound. 'Knock! Knock! Open the Door' by Michaela Morgan and David Walker might have a tulip block or rhythm sticks to bang together. 'Three Little Pigs' might have a drum or tambour to represent the wolf knocking on the door. Seat the children in a circle with one child as the listener sat in the middle. (Ask the listener to close her eyes or wear a blindfold if she is comfortable with this.) Tell the story and help each child to make a sound in the right place. The child in the middle must point to the child who she thinks made the sound. They then swap places and the story continues.

Section 5: Finding Sound

☐ *Think of a story*

Repeat the 'Sound in stories' activity, but this time help the children to make up their own story. Let them choose the sound makers.

 Always be extremely cautious when carrying out activities where the child has her eyes closed or is blindfolded.

FINDING SOUND: MUSICAL INSTRUMENTS
Activities for Home

These games will help your child learn to locate sounds. Your child will enjoy listening for the musical instruments. Make sure the room is as quiet as possible.

☐ Who's that?

Play this game with another adult. Both adults should have a musical toy, such as maracas, rattles or sleigh bells. Sit on one side of your child; the other person should sit on the other side. Take it in turns to make a sound. When your child turns to the sound, let her play with the toy.

☐ Turn to the sound

Play this game with your child using a drum or other musical instrument. Stand behind her and make a sound with the instrument. Does she turn to the sound? At first, she may need prompting. You could call her name and make the sound again when she turns.

Perhaps another child or adult could be a helper. They should sit in front of the child and prompt her to turn. They can also keep your child's attention and stop her from turning before you make the sound.

☐ Hide the music

Play hiding games with your child. Use a musical instrument like a bell or tambourine, and hide with it somewhere in the room. Make a continuous or repetitive sound. Can your child find you by listening for that sound?

☐ Where's the music box?

Hide a music box in the room. Can your child find it by listening for the sound? Use a music box that only plays for a short time. Your child will have to be quick to find the box before the music stops.

FINDING SOUND
Sound Makers and Musical Instruments

Try using a variety of musical instruments or music makers to play finding sound games. Choose ones that make a continuous or repetitive sound. Here are some suggestions:

- ☐ sleigh bells
- ☐ hand held bells
- ☐ squeaker
- ☐ tambourine
- ☐ drum
- ☐ rattle
- ☐ maraca
- ☐ rhythm sticks
- ☐ music box

FINDING SOUND: ANIMAL SOUNDS
Teaching Activity

'Farmer Find Your Animals'

You will need;
a large floor space where the children can sit in a circle.

Useful words and phrases:
listen; look; close your eyes; farmer; name of animal; where is the . . .?; who made the sound?.

What to do:

1. Seat the children in a circle on the floor or on chairs. Explain that they are going to be playing a listening game. (It is important that the children are able to recognize animal sounds, as well as being able to make sounds, before they try this activity. You may like to spend some time practising this before you start.)

2. Choose one child as the farmer and ask her to stand in the middle of the circle and close her eyes. (She can wear a blindfold if she is agreeable, or you could ask all the children in the outer circle to put their heads down so their faces are hidden.)

3. One child in the circle is chosen to be an animal, such as a cow. (Let the group decide which animal.)

4. She must wait for the child in the centre to say, "Where are you, cow?" before she makes a cow sound.

5. The farmer in the middle must point to where the noise is coming from. If the farmer is unsure, let her see the location of the sound and listen again.

6. When the animal is found, she joins the farmer in the middle.

7. The game continues with a different child until the farmer collects all the animals.

To increase the complexity of the activity

- ask the child to make the animal sound quieter;
- increase the distance between the animal and the farmer;
- have fewer repetitions of the animal sounds.

Section 5: Finding Sound

Variations

- The child in the circle chooses an animal sound to make, but does not tell anyone the animal. The 'farmer' has to guess the animal as well as point to the sound. (Remember that the child must be at the stage to recognize and name animal sounds.)
- The farmer is given a picture of an animal. When she hears the sound of the animal, she must give the picture to the child she thinks is making the sound.
- Give the farmer a picture of an animal; this time two or three different animal sounds are made. The farmer must wait till she hears the sound of the animal in the picture before she points to the sound. (The children should be familiar with the teaching activity before attempting this game.)

FINDING SOUND: ANIMAL SOUNDS
Activities for Early Years Settings

These activities help the children to develop skills in locating sound. They will enjoy the animal theme.

❑ *Dangerous animals*

Sit one child on a chair. On either side of her, behind screens, are two other children. Explain to the children that the screens are rocks and a dangerous animal might be hiding behind them. (Be careful that the screens are not so thick that they muffle the sound.) Tell the child seated in the middle to listen very carefully. If she hears the sound of an animal, she must point to where she thinks it is hiding. Signal to one of the children behind the rocks to make a sound. If the child points at the correct rock, the child who is hiding can leap out and make a frightening animal noise.

❑ *Lost animals*

One child is chosen to pretend to be a lost animal. She moves quietly round the room crying plaintively every now and then. How long is it before the blindfolded 'owner' can find her by pointing to the sound?

❑ *'Lost kitty'*

Play 'Lost kitty'. One child closes her eyes while another child is chosen as the kitten and hides somewhere in the room. The first child opens her eyes and calls for the 'kitten', who 'miaows' loudly until she is found.

❑ *Here, chick chick!*

You will need several blank pictures, two or three pictures of chicks and one picture of a hen. The children each select a picture without letting the other children see them. The child with the hen picture leaves the room. The other children form a circle, including the two or three children who have pictures of chicks. When the hen returns, all the children put their heads down. (This way the hen will not see who is making the noise.) The hen calls to her chicks with a cluck. The chicks reply with a chirp-chirp. The hen must point to those children she thinks are the chicks.

❑ *Sound in stories*

Select a story that provides plenty of opportunity for making animal sounds. 'Dear Zoo' by Rod Campbell and 'Brown Bear, Brown Bear, What Do You See?' by Bill Martin are good books for this activity. Seat

Section 5: Finding Sound

the children in a circle with one child as the listener sat in the middle. (Ask the listener to close her eyes or wear a blindfold if she is comfortable with this.) Tell the story and help different children to make an animal sound in the right place. It might help to give the child an animal picture or toy to help them remember. The child in the middle must point to the child who she thinks made the sound. They then swap places and the story continues.

 Always be extremely cautious when carrying out activities where the child has her eyes closed or is blindfolded.

FINDING SOUND: ANIMAL SOUNDS
Activities for Home

These activities use animal sounds to help your child learn to locate sound. She will enjoy hearing and making the different sounds.

❏ *Hide-and-seek*

Pretend to be an animal. Hide somewhere in the room while your child closes her eyes. Make an animal sound. Can your child find you? Ask her to hide and make an animal noise for you to find her.

❏ *Animal faces*

Play hide-and-seek as in the previous activity, but wear an animal face that matches the sound you are making. Jump out when your child finds you and mime the animal.

❏ *Farm or zoo visit*

At the farm or zoo, talk to your child about the different animal sounds she can hear around her. As you walk around, draw her attention to the sounds of animals that you can hear but which are out of sight. Ask her what she can hear? Ask her to point to where she thinks they are. Go and see if she is right. Which animal does she think is the noisiest? The monkey house is usually pretty noisy.

❏ *Everyday animals*

Listen for animal sounds when you are walking with your child in the park or along the street. Tell her if you hear a dog barking or a cat miaowing. Ask her what is making the sound, and where the dog or cat is that made the sound.

❏ *'Moo, cow, moo' party game*

Use the commercially made 'Tin Animal Sound Makers'. These make the sound of a cow, a pig or a sheep when tipped over. One child plays the farmer who needs to find his lost cows. One blindfolded child (the farmer) sits in the middle of a small circle of children, while another child from the circle is chosen to be the 'cow' and is given the 'cow' sound maker. The 'cow' must wait for the child in the middle to call out "moo, cow, moo" before she makes the noise. If the child in the middle is successful at pointing to the 'cow', they swap places. (Make sure the children are well spaced out for this activity.)

 Always be extremely cautious when carrying out activities where the child has her eyes closed or is blindfolded.

FINDING SOUND
Animal Sound Makers

The following toys can be used to represent animal noises:

- ❏ cuddly animal toys
- ❏ plastic animal shapes
- ❏ pictures or photographs of animals
- ❏ animal masks
- ❏ miniature animals
- ❏ animal puppets

Below is a suggested list of animal sounds to use in sound location activities. Remember EAL learners may use different sounds to represent animals. These sounds can be listed under 'alternative sounds' as a reference for adults when planning activities.

			Alternative sounds
❏	cat	miaow	
❏	dog	woof woof	
❏	bird	cheep, chirp	
❏	parrot	squawk	
❏	cow	moo	
❏	pig	oink	
❏	duck	quack	
❏	horse	neigh	
❏	sheep	baah	
❏	chicken	cluck	
❏	cockerel	cock-a-doodle-doo	
❏	bear	growl	
❏	monkey	oo-oo	
❏	lion	roar	

FINDING SOUND: ACTION SOUNDS
Teaching Activity

'Don't Wake the Monster'

You will need:
a large floor space.

Useful words and phrases:
listen; don't wake the monster!; quietly; where is the noise?

What to do:

1. This activity is best when played with a group of children in a large, roomy area, which is quiet and free from interruptions.

2. One child is chosen to be the 'monster'. Ask her to stand in the centre of the room with her eyes closed or wearing a blindfold if she is comfortable with this. The other children take up positions around the room, being careful to leave spaces between themselves.

3. One child is instructed to start moving around the room when the adult points at her. She must be as quiet as possible, so as not to wake the monster.

4. If she is able to get round the room without being caught by the monster, another child takes her place.

5. The child in the centre must listen very carefully for the sound of any movement. If she hears any movement, she must point in the direction of the noise. (As children always find it difficult to keep quiet, the child will soon give herself away. Other children must be warned that they will be 'out' if they make a noise.)

6. If the child is unsure or makes a mistake, let her see where the noise is coming from. (Hold her hand so that she can compare where the sound is to where she pointed.)

7. If the child in the middle is correct, she swaps places with the other child, who then becomes the monster.

Section 5: Finding Sound

To increase the complexity of the activity

◆ increase the distance between the child in the middle and the children around her.

Variations

◆ Children take turns to do an action, such as stamping their feet or clapping their hands. The child in the middle has to locate the sound and copy the action before they can swap places.

◆ The children are asked to carry something that makes a noise, like a maraca or rattle.

FINDING SOUND: ACTION SOUNDS
Activities for Early Years Settings

These activities help the children with locating sound made at a distance. They are particularly suited for physical play. Remember to keep background noise to a minimum.

☐ *Find that action*

One child is chosen to stand in the centre of the room with her eyes closed or wearing a blindfold if she is agreeable. The other children take up positions around the room, being careful to leave spaces between themselves. The children take it in turns to do an action, such as stamping their feet or clapping their hands. The child in the middle has to locate the sound and copy the action. If she is right, she can swap places with the other child.

☐ *Sound obstacle course*

You will need to set up a sound obstacle course. Place items on the course that will make it difficult for the child to be quiet: for example, crawling under a line hung with noisy paper. (See other ideas for an obstacle course on p. 97.) One child is chosen as the listener and must close her eyes or wear a blindfold if she is comfortable with this. She must try to catch the other children passing round the obstacle course by pointing in the direction of any sounds she hears. (To stop any cheating, she must say what she has heard before she looks.) If she is right, the other child is 'out' and they swap places.

☐ *Catch the sound*

Play this game with two or three children, or more if you have the space. In this activity all the children except one are seated with heads down and eyes closed. The remaining child is given something noisy to hold or wear, such as a cowbell on a necklace. (Avoid anything with jingle bells or jingles, as they are very difficult to keep quiet.) She must walk around the room without making a sound. The other children try to catch her by pointing in the direction of any sounds they hear.

There are lots of party games that involve sound location. See 'Activities for Home' for suitable games.

 Always be extremely cautious when carrying out activities where the child has her eyes closed or is blindfolded.

FINDING SOUND: ACTION SOUNDS
Activities for Home

There are lots of traditional party games that involve finding sound. These games need to be played where there is plenty of space.

☐ 'Blind man's buff'

One child is blindfolded. The other children move around. The blindfolded child tries to catch the other children by listening for any movements.

☐ Grandmother's footsteps

One child plays grandmother. She stands facing one wall. All the other children stand on the other side of the room. They must try to creep up and touch grandmother. If grandmother hears a sound, she can turn round towards the sound. Any child still moving is out of the game.

☐ Dragon's treasure

The children try to steal the dragon's treasure. Choose a child to be the dragon. She must sit with her eyes closed, or blindfolded if she is comfortable with this, in the middle of the room. The other children must try to creep up and steal the treasure. (Chocolate gold coins make a good prize for a party.) If the dragon hears a sound, she must point in the direction of the noise. Any child caught trying to steal the treasure is out of the game. Instead of a dragon, you could have a king, queen, pirate, monster or giant.

 Always be extremely cautious when carrying out activities where the child has her eyes closed or is blindfolded.

FINDING SOUND
Action Sounds

Some suitable action sounds might include:

- ❑ clapping
- ❑ stamping feet
- ❑ banging
- ❑ knocking
- ❑ tapping foot
- ❑ drumming fingers

Ideas for a 'sound' obstacle course include:

- ❑ walking through dried leaves
- ❑ climbing through a hoop with bells or crunchy paper tied around it
- ❑ crawling along a plastic tunnel
- ❑ jumping from one hoop (laid on the floor) to another
- ❑ carrying a bell
- ❑ wearing noisy bracelets or anklets
- ❑ crawling under a line hung with noisy paper

FINDING SOUND: ENVIRONMENTAL SOUNDS
Teaching Activity

'Stop and Listen'

You will need:
access to a large hall or outside space.

Useful words and phrases:
listen; look; what do you hear?; where is the sound?; near; far; point to the sound?

(N.B. Children must have been successful at the previous teaching activities in this section before attempting this activity.)

What to do:

1. Go to the middle of the school hall or main nursery corridor and tell the children to listen to the noises around them.

2. Talk about the noises they can hear.

3. Choose one of the children to listen. Ask her to close her eyes and tell you the first sound that she hears. Then ask her to point in the direction of the sound.

4. Keep her hand pointing in that direction by holding it, so that she can compare this with where the actual sound source is located. When she has located the sound, encourage her to close her eyes and listen again.

5. Continue until all the children have had a turn.

6. Next repeat the activity, but this time when the child has her eyes closed, spin her around to disorient her. (Warn her first!) So now, if the child recognizes a sound, such as saucepans banging, she will have to listen and not use her knowledge of the location of the kitchens.

7. Let her see where she has pointed, and compare this with where the sound is located.

8. When she has localized the sound source, encourage her to close her eyes and listen again.

9. Continue until all the children have had a turn.

To increase the complexity of the activity

- ask the children to locate sounds that are quiet or far away;
- ask the child to locate less familiar sounds;
- ask the child to locate a familiar sound in an unfamiliar place.

Variation

- Split the group into two teams. The winners are the team that has the most correct 'finds'.

 Always be extremely cautious when carrying out activities where the child has her eyes closed or is blindfolded.

FINDING SOUND: ENVIRONMENTAL SOUNDS

Activities for Early Years Settings

These activities encourage the children to think about the sounds they hear around them in their environment. They also help to develop the children's skills for locating sound sources.

Listen to the sounds

Ask the children to close their eyes and listen to the sounds around them. Ask them what they can hear. Can they point in the direction of the sounds?

Symbols

Older children can play this game. Draw three symbols on a chart, for example, three stars in a row. Place a counter on the middle symbol. Seat two children so that they are on either side of the child but out of her sight. They take turns to make a sound using a desk bell or buzzer. (Make sure they avoid a pattern, such as right, left, right, left, otherwise the child in the middle will be able to anticipate the direction of the sound.) The child in the middle moves the counter to the symbol on the right or left, depending on the direction of the sound.

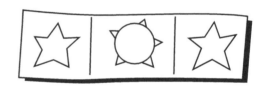

Near and far games

Ask the children to close their eyes and listen to the sounds around them. What sounds can they hear? Where are the sounds? Can they tell you which sounds are near and which ones are far? Ask them to point to different near and far sounds.

Section 5: Finding Sound

☐ *Match the picture to the sound*

Try this activity with those children who are able to recognize sounds. Have two or three pictures of everyday objects. Hide in the room one object represented in the pictures. Ask one of the children to point to the sound. Before they find the object, they must point to the picture of the object they think is making the sound.

FINDING SOUND: ENVIRONMENTAL SOUNDS
Activities for Home

These activities will help your child to be more aware of sounds in her immediate environment. They will also help to develop her skills in finding sound.

☐ *Daily sounds around us*

During the day, talk about the sounds your child can hear around her but that are not in immediate sight. Encourage her to find out who or what is making the sound. Try to choose something that will have an intrinsic reward for her, for example: the ping of the microwave after cooking popcorn. Talk about where the sound is made, for example, in the kitchen.

☐ *Hide-and-seek*

Play the traditional game of hide and seek in the garden or at your local park, but introduce some sound by clapping, singing or calling your child's name. (Warn her first before you disappear!) Can she find you? Swap over and let her hide from you.

☐ *Where is the sound?*

You will need two boxes and an everyday object that makes a loud noise, such as an alarm clock or musical toy. Show your child the two empty boxes. Explain that you are going to hide the object in one of the boxes. Tell her to close her eyes. Put the object in one of the boxes and place it to one side of the child. Place the other box on the other side of her. Ask her to open her eyes and listen. Can she point to the box that has the sound maker inside?

FINDING SOUND
Environmental Sounds

Here are some suggestions for common sounds in the environment:

Home sounds

- ☐ phone
- ☐ washing machine
- ☐ microwave pinging
- ☐ baby cries
- ☐ doorbell

- ☐ door knocker/bell
- ☐ alarm clock
- ☐ pet noises, e.g. barking, miaowing

Nursery or school sounds

- ☐ playground bell
- ☐ whistle
- ☐ piano
- ☐ singing
- ☐ PE or sports sounds

- ☐ children playing, e.g. toy bricks dropping
- ☐ kitchen sounds
- ☐ playground noises, such as games, skipping songs

Outside

- ☐ aeroplane
- ☐ train
- ☐ bus horn
- ☐ car horn
- ☐ motorbike

- ☐ bike bell
- ☐ wheels on a skateboard
- ☐ dog barking
- ☐ children playing

FINDING SOUND
Record Sheet

Child's name	

Date	Activity/Context	Observations
Example 3.7.	**Played 'Match the picture to the sound' with one other child. Using two everyday objects (alarm clock and CD player). (AI)**	**(Child's name) picked up the picture of the alarm clock when she heard it ring. She pointed to the side of the room where the clock was hidden and found the clock with the help of the assistant.**

AI = adult initiated activity; CI = child initiated activity

SECTION 6
Volume and Pitch

Introduction.. 107

Listening to Loud and Quiet in Musical Instruments.. 108

  Teaching Activity 108

  Activities for Early Years Settings...................................110

  Activities for Home...112

  Musical Instruments 113

Listening to High and Low in Musical Instruments...114

  Teaching Activity 114

  Activities for Early Years Settings...................................116

  Activities for Home...118

  Musical Instruments 120

Record Sheet.. 121

INTRODUCTION

The *activities* in this section help develop fine discrimination skills. They focus on two characteristics of sound: volume and pitch, which are demonstrated using musical instruments.

Children with a hearing loss often have difficulty in discriminating these characteristics, and they will benefit from focused listening practice. The activities can also be used to help concentration and memory skills in children with other communication difficulties.

Some children may be able to discriminate these characteristics without being able to identify the sound, for example: they may know when a drumbeat is loud and when it is quiet, but not the name of the instrument. So activities are designed so that the children are only required to learn to respond to changes in volume and pitch.

For older children, the concepts and vocabulary of volume and pitch can be introduced.

VOLUME AND PITCH: LISTENING TO LOUD AND QUIET IN MUSICAL INSTRUMENTS

Teaching Activity

'Beat that drum'

You will need:
two drums; a screen; two beaters.

Useful words and phrases:
look, listen; drum; quiet, loud; wait.

What to do:

1. You will need two drums and two beaters. First let the child explore making some sounds with one of the drums and one of the beaters.

2. Tell the child that you are going to make a loud noise with the drum. Beat the drum several times, and then help her to copy you in making a loud noise. Talk to her about how the sound is loud. (Use gesture or sign if appropriate.)

3. Encourage her to copy you in making another loud sound.

4. Tell the child that you are going to make a quiet noise with the drum. (Again use gesture or sign if appropriate.) Encourage her to copy you in making a quiet noise.

5. Explain to the child that you are going to play a listening game. This time have another identical drum for yourself. Let her see you make the sounds at first, so that the strength of arm movement is a clue. Make a loud sound on your drum and help her copy you on her drum.

7. When she is consistent in responding, try hiding your drum behind a screen.

8. Continue the game with the child listening alone. (Some children may need to hear the loud sound played two or three times *before* they are able to copy.)

9. Continue the game making loud and quiet sounds.

To increase the complexity of the activity

- use fewer repetitions of the drum beat;
- make the difference in volume between the drums narrower;
- introduce a delay before the child is allowed to respond.

Variations

- Vary the musical instruments.
- Let the child make sounds for you to copy. Give her feedback on whether they were loud or quiet.

VOLUME AND PITCH: LISTENING TO LOUD AND QUIET IN MUSICAL INSTRUMENTS

Activities for Early Years Settings

Vary the instruments you use but make sure you only use one instrument in each game. If the instruments are different, the children may be responding to the different sounds and not to a difference in volume. Use gestures or sign if appropriate to indicate loud and quiet, if the children are unsure of the words.

 It is important to check that loud sounds are comfortable for children and that the quiet sounds are audible.

▢ *Movement to music*

Play loud and quiet sounds using a musical instrument like a drum, tambour or piano. Get the children to move according to the volume of the music. A loud tune may have large steps with stamping feet and big arm movements. A quiet tune may have little skips, walking on tiptoe or gentle swaying.

▢ *Put a counter on the loud sound*

Play this game with individual children. Make a lotto card with a big circle and a small circle marked on it. You will also need several counters. Use a musical instrument like a maraca to make loud and quiet sounds out of sight. When the child hears a loud sound, she must place a counter on the big circle. When the child hears a quiet sound, she must place a counter on the small circle.

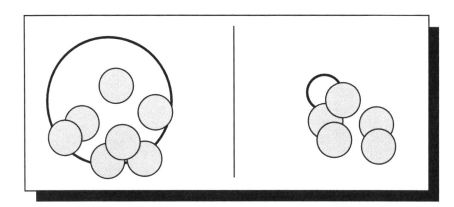

Section 6: Volume and Pitch

☐ *Sesame Street lullaby*

This is a great video to prompt a discussion about loud and quiet. Be warned it is very 'loud' in parts!

Available at https://www.youtube.com/watch?v=Jc20vMz0V7Q

Extend this activity by using lullabies from diverse cultures. Ask families for suggestions or recordings of family members singing.

☐ *Team games*

Use a drum for this game. Divide the children into two teams. One team is told to listen for a loud sound and the other to listen for a quiet sound. Demonstrate the two sounds on the drum. The teams can only move across the room when they hear their sound played. (The children could hop or skip.) When the sound changes, they must stop and wait until they hear their sound again. The winning team is the first to cross the room.

☐ *Make a headband*

Give the child a strip of card and a crayon or paint marker. (Something she feels comfortable using to make marks.) Explain that when she hears a loud sound, she must make a big dot on the card, and when she hears a quiet sound, she must make a small dot. The card can be used to make a headband.

Make different patterns by using different shapes and colours. Use big and small stamper markers to make small and big circles, stars or hearts. The strips of card can be made into headbands, bracelets or necklaces by joining the ends with sticky tape. Other sizes and shapes of cards can be used to make badges, belts and book covers.

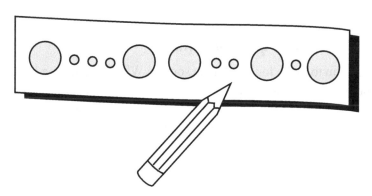

☐ *Quiet and loud sounds*

Ask the children to close their eyes and listen to the sounds around them. What sounds can they hear? Can they tell you which sounds are quiet and which ones are loud? The children can make a list of quiet sounds and a list of loud sounds. Does everybody agree that the sounds are quiet or loud? Ask the children to point to different quiet and loud sounds.

☐ *Sounds in the environment*

Repeat the earlier activities in various settings and ask the children to compare the different noises. Do sounds change from quiet to loud in different settings? Discuss why changes in our perception of loudness occur in different settings, such as a cough in the street compared with a cough in a library.

VOLUME AND PITCH: LISTENING TO LOUD AND QUIET IN MUSICAL INSTRUMENTS

Activities for Home

These activities will help your child in listening for loud and quiet sounds in musical instruments. Reduce the volume if your child finds the level of sound uncomfortable. Experiment with how loud a sound needs to be for it to be audible to your child.

☐ *Copy a loud sound*

Experiment with making different sounds by beating on a drum or up turned bucket with a stick. See if you can make some loud and quiet sounds. Help your child to copy the sounds you make. Talk about how some sounds are loud and some are quiet. Ask her which sounds she likes best.

☐ *Movement to music*

Play loud and quiet music by turning the volume up and down. Show your child how to take large steps to a loud tune and little skipping movements to a quiet tune.

☐ *Loud and quiet animals*

Use a drum to make loud and quiet sounds. When you make a loud sound, encourage your child to be a large animal like an elephant. She can sway to the loud beat of the drum and take big steps around the room. When you play a quiet sound, she can be a small animal like a mouse and make little tiptoe movements.

☐ *Hot and cold*

You will need a maraca, shaker or rattle for this game. Hide an object from your child in the room. To help her to find it, you can give her a clue using your instrument. Play a loud sound as she nears the object. Play quieter sounds if she moves away from it.

VOLUME AND PITCH: LISTENING TO LOUD AND QUIET IN MUSICAL INSTRUMENTS
Musical Instruments

A variety of musical instruments and sound makers can be used in games using loud and quiet sounds. Remember that pitch can vary even in the same type of instrument and be an extra cue. Try to use one musical instrument for each game. Your choice might include some of the following:

- ❏ wood blocks and mallet
- ❏ rhythm sticks
- ❏ drum
- ❏ tambourine
- ❏ maracas
- ❏ shaker
- ❏ piano
- ❏ bell

Homemade musical instruments

- ❏ empty biscuit tin and a wooden spoon (drum)
- ❏ sticks and an upturned bucket (drum)
- ❏ frying pan or saucepan lid (gong)
- ❏ two sticks to tap together (rhythm sticks)

VOLUME AND PITCH: LISTENING TO HIGH AND LOW IN MUSICAL INSTRUMENTS
Teaching Activity

'Chime bar steps'

You will need:
two chime bar steps
with eight coloured chime bars;
two beaters; a screen.

Useful words and phrases:
look, listen; chime bar; wait; low; high; hide; names of colours.

What to do:

1. The chime bar step is a visual aid to the change in pitch as it represents the idea of a staircase. Choose two chime bars, one that would go on the bottom step and one on the top stair (that is the lowest and the highest sounds).

2. First let the child explore making some sounds with the low-pitched chime bar and one of the mallets. Give her one of the chime bar steps.

3. When the child has finished playing, put this chime bar on the lowest step, and introduce the high-pitched chime bar. Let the child have a turn at playing with this one, and then place it on the highest step.

4. Make a sound with the low-pitched chime bar, talk about the colour and length of the bar. Compare this with the colour and length of the high-pitched chime bar so the child can see this is shorter and a different colour. Introduce the terms high and low. A raised hand can be used to indicate a high-pitched sound and a lowered hand to indicate a low-pitched sound.

5. Explain to the child that you are going to play a listening game. Place a chime bar step in front of the child and have one for yourself. Place one of the low-pitched chime bars in front of the child. Play a sound on your low-pitched chime bar. Can she copy you? Then place it on the bottom step. Can the child do the same with her steps? Repeat with the high-pitched sound.

Section 6: Volume and Pitch

6 Next introduce the screen. Make sure the child is ready, and then tell her to listen carefully. Make a sound with the low-pitched chime bar. Can she copy you with her low-pitched chime bar?

7 Give feedback by showing her your chime bar on the steps and repeating the sound. Repeat the activity with the high-pitched chime bar.

8 Practise this activity until the child is confident with discriminating between high and low. Remember some children will need lots of practice watching and listening before they move to listening alone.

To increase the complexity of the activity

- use fewer repetitions on the chime bar;
- make the difference in pitch between the two chime bars narrower;
- introduce a delay before the child is allowed to respond.

Variations

- Ask the child to make the sounds for you to copy.
- Vary the musical instruments.

VOLUME AND PITCH: LISTENING TO HIGH AND LOW IN MUSICAL INSTRUMENTS

Activities for Early Years Settings

These activities help the children to practise their skills in discriminating high and low sounds in musical instruments. Vary the instruments you use but make sure you only use one instrument in each game: if the instruments are different, the children may be responding to the different sounds and not to a difference in pitch. Use hand gestures to indicate high and low if the children are unsure of the words.

☐ Post it game

You will need two boxes and two chime bars that have a high and a low-pitched note. Place one box high up (for the high sound) and one low down (for the low sound). The child posts an object in the appropriate box when she hears a sound from the chime bars.

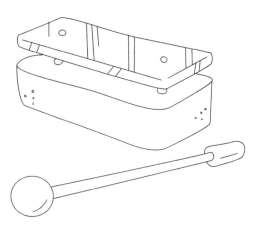

☐ Action and movement game

This game is more fun with a group of children. You will need a musical instrument that plays low and high notes: for example, a two tone block where you can also show the difference in length between the blocks relative to the pitch. Play a low note and encourage the children to crouch on the floor. Play a high note and encourage the children to stand on tiptoe with their arms stretched above their head. Hide the instrument and play different notes, alternating between high and low. Can the children match their actions to the different pitch levels?

☐ Bird in the tree

You will need a xylophone to play a high and a low-pitched note. Hang up a picture of a tree, and have some cut-out birds. When the child hears

Section 6: Volume and Pitch

a high sound, she can hang a bird on the top part of the tree. (Use some re-usable adhesive like Blu Tack.) When she hears a low sound, she can place a bird on the ground. See if the child can make a finer discrimination between different pitch levels. Make a very high note for the crown of the tree and a high note for the top half of the tree. Make a very low note for the ground and a low note for the bottom half of the tree.

☐ *Bridges*

Use a double agogo bell. Show the child how the bells have different lengths and sizes related to the high and low pitch. Either draw or make two bridges with several cardboard cut-outs of vehicles such as cars, buses, motorbikes and caravans. Place one bridge higher than the other. When the child hears a high sound from the agogo bell, she must place a vehicle on the high bridge. When she hears a low sound from the bell, she must place a vehicle on the low bridge. (Other instruments can be substituted for this game.)

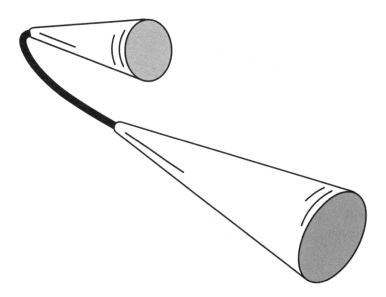

VOLUME AND PITCH: LISTENING TO HIGH AND LOW IN MUSICAL INSTRUMENTS
Activities for Home

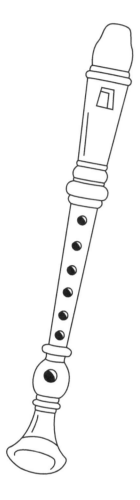

These activities will help your child in listening for high and low sounds in musical instruments. Only use one instrument in each game, otherwise your child may be responding to the different instruments and not to a difference in the sound. Use hand gestures to indicate high and low if your child is unsure of the words.

☐ *Exploring high and low notes*

Use a recorder to show your child how to experiment with making high and low sounds. Let her make some sounds. When she plays a high note, stand on tip-toe and raise your hands above your head. When she plays a low note, crouch down on the floor. Stand with knees bent for notes in the middle. Play some notes for your child. Can she make the appropriate actions?

☐ *Swanee slide whistle*

This is a super toy for exploring changes in pitch. You may be familiar with the sound from the children's television programme 'The Clangers'. This is like a whistle, except that it has a sliding piece, which can be moved up and down inside to vary the tone. You and your child will enjoy experimenting with making the different sounds.

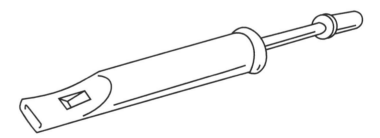

☐ *Water flutes*

Play with some water flutes at bath time. Fill these colourful flutes with different amounts of water to play a range of different notes.

Section 6: Volume and Pitch

☐ *Hoop-la*

Play this version of 'hoop-la'. Your child must throw the ring onto a high peg when you play a high sound and onto a low peg for a low sound. Use two different chords on the same instrument to make the sounds (xylophone or glockenspiel). Start with two sounds that are very dissimilar. (If you do not have hoop-la, use tennis or small balls with boxes placed at different heights.)

☐ *Going up, going down*

Draw a picture of a tall block of flats. Give your child a counter or toy brick to move up and down as a lift. A recorder or swanee whistle are good instruments for this game. When the instrument makes a high note, the lift goes to the top floor. When the instrument plays a low note, it goes to the bottom floor. (Try this game using a rocket, the rising moon or a fire fighter climbing a ladder.)

VOLUME AND PITCH: LISTENING TO HIGH AND LOW IN MUSICAL INSTRUMENTS
Musical Instruments

A variety of musical instruments or music makers can be used for listening to high and low sounds; for example:

- ❏ metal chime bars
- ❏ wooden chime bars
- ❏ glockenspiel
- ❏ xylophone
- ❏ piano
- ❏ guitar
- ❏ swanee whistle
- ❏ water flutes
- ❏ recorder
- ❏ two tone blocks
- ❏ double agogo bell

VOLUME AND PITCH
Record Sheet

Child's name	

Date	Activity/Context	Observations
Example 30.5.	Working with teaching assistant in a one:one session. Teaching activity on discriminating pitch using chime bar steps. (AI)	Able to copy playing high and low notes. Placed chime bars in correct position on steps. Made sounds when chime bar was hidden out of sight. With several repetitions she was able to match the pitch.

AI = adult initiated activity; CI = child initiated activity

SECTION 7
Rhythm and Sequencing

Introduction 125

Listening to the Beat 126

    Teaching Activity 126

    Activities for Early Years Settings 128

    Activities for Home 130

    Musical Instruments 131

Listening to Long and Short 132

    Teaching Activity 132

    Activities for Early Years Settings 133

    Activities for Home 134

    Musical Instruments 135

Listening to Fast and Slow 136

    Teaching Activity 136

Activities for Early Years Settings................................ 137

Activities for Home...................................... 138

Musical Instruments 139

Generalization of Rhythm Skills............................ 140

Sequencing Sounds.. 141

Teaching Activity 141

Activities for Early Years Settings................................ 143

Activities for Home...................................... 144

Musical Instruments 145

Record Sheet... 146

INTRODUCTION

The ability to copy a rhythm and recall the order of sounds presented in a sequence are important aspects in the development of the child's auditory skills. Children with a hearing loss often have difficulty in sequencing sounds and speech. The activities in this section will help the child to practise skills such as memory and ordering through the use of non-speech sounds. Many of the activities in other sections can also be modified to teach sequencing.

Identifying and imitating rhythms involves anticipation and recall. These skills will be utilized by the child when she later needs to sequence and order sounds into patterns. The following activities involve the senses of sight, hearing and touch. The child will learn to integrate what she sees, hears and feels and reproduce this through an action or movement.

RHYTHM AND SEQUENCING: LISTENING TO THE BEAT
Teaching Activities

'Beat Out That Rhythm'

You will need:
two drums.

Useful words and phrases:
look; listen; drum(s);
copy; beat; one; two; three.

What to do:

1. Explain to the child that you are going to play a listening game.

2. It is important to start with the child copying rhythms using her dominant side, whether this is right or left. Try to use the same hand as the child.

3. Let her watch as you beat out a pattern on one of the drums. Start with two beats (da-da).

4. Encourage the child to copy the beats using the other drum.

5. If she has difficulty, check that she can copy one beat and then, if necessary, physically manipulate her hands to beat out two beats. It may be necessary for you to use one drum and for you to beat out the rhythm together.

6. Once the child is confident in imitating two beats, you can introduce three beats (da-da-da).

7. Keep the beats evenly spaced and regular.

8. When the child is competent beating the rhythm alongside you, let her watch you and then try on her own.

To increase the complexity of the activity

- increase the number of beats in the rhythm;
- ask the child to listen with her eyes closed and then beat out the pattern;
- ask the child to use both hands; two hands on one drum or two drums;
- ask the child to alternate rhythms from one side to the other, for example right to left to right to left.

Variations

- Vary the musical instruments.
- Ask the child to carry out an action each time you beat the drum, for example to raise her arms.

RHYTHM AND SEQUENCING: LISTENING TO THE BEAT

Activities for Early Years Settings

These games will help children to develop simple rhythms. Keep the beats evenly spaced and of equal length. At first, let the children watch as you beat out the patterns; later, they can try the activities with listening alone. There is a mixture of activities for individual child, pairs or groups of children.

☐ Action to the beat

Beat out a single rhythm using a tambourine (for example, da–da–da). On each beat the children must carry out an action, such as waving. Let the children take turns to play the rhythm for the other children.

☐ Mark a pattern

Give the child some paint markers and some paper. Ask her to make a mark each time you play a beat on a drum.

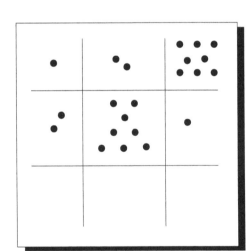

☐ Rhythm lotto

Play this game using a xylophone or chime bar to make sounds. Draw a lotto card with nine squares and six blank cards. Mark in each square a dot to represent different numbers of beats on an instrument. So one dot indicates one note, two dots indicate two notes, several dots indicate several notes. The child listens and covers a square when she hears the beat. The last line of the lotto card can be left blank for the child to complete. (See illustration.) Marking one dot for one beat, two dots for two beats and so on.

☐ Copy this beat

This is a barrier game for two children. Use a drum to show the children how to play a simple two-beat rhythm, such as da–da, and a three-beat one. Have cards to illustrate the pattern: for example, two dots, three dots. Ask each child to have a turn at copying it. Provide two drums and a screen. Provide different cards with different rhythm patterns for each child. Let the children play rhythms for each other to copy. Can the children copy the rhythm correctly when they are relying on listening alone?

☐ Movement to the beat

Try these different movement games with the children.

You will need lots of space. They involve listening to the number of beats. Use a drum to beat out the rhythm:

Section 7: Rhythm and Sequencing

one beat played slowly – the children must walk slowly until you say "Stop";

two beats in quick succession – the children must walk quickly until you say "Stop".

Alternatively, ask the children to shuffle across the room. When you play some beats on the drum they must stop and carry out the appropriate action:

one beat – jump one-quarter of a circle (so they are facing sideways);

two beats – two quarter jumps (so they should be facing back where they came from);

three beats – three jumps that form three-quarters of a circle;

four beats – four jumps that should bring the child in a full circle to face the front. Anybody facing the wrong way is 'out'.

In between beats they continue to shuffle across the room, but each time they will be going in a different direction.

▢ *Following a pattern*

A group of children can play this game and get lots of listening practice. Draw a pattern of dots on a long strip of card. Choose one child to beat out the rhythm for the other children to mark out the pattern on individual cards. They can check their finished designs against the original pattern. Use several different designs so that each child in the group has a turn at beating out the rhythm.

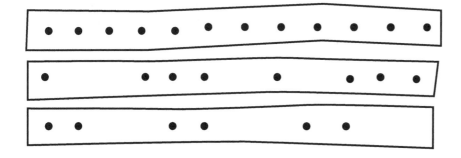

RHYTHM AND SEQUENCING: LISTENING TO THE BEAT
Activities for Home

These activities will help your child to copy simple rhythms using musical instruments.

☐ *Beat the drum*

You will need a drum and two beaters (or two sticks and an upturned box or bucket). Show your child a simple rhythm of two beats on the drum (da–da). Can she copy you, using her beater? Encourage her to play along with you. Increase the number of beats, but keep them evenly spaced (da–da–da). Can she copy the rhythm?

☐ *Clapping games*

Use your hands to make music by playing clapping games. Can she copy a simple rhythm by clapping her hands together? Can she clap her hands above her head, behind her knees and over her shoulder?

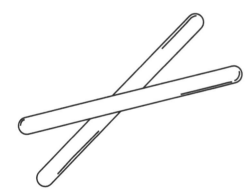

☐ *Tap out that rhythm*

Walk round the house and tap different objects. (Use a wooden spoon or stick.) Ask your child to tap them with the same number of beats. Some may have two beats (da–da) others three (da–da–da). Encourage your child to keep the beats even. When your child is confident with this game, try tapping out a rhythm with both hands. You could use two sticks to tap out the beat on the same object, or tap twice on one object with one hand and twice on another with the other hand.

☐ *Shake the beat*

Play some instrumental music that has a steady beat. You will need two maracas or homemade shakers. Help your child to copy you as you follow the beat with your sound maker. You can gently tap the shaker against the palm of your hand, on your shoe, or on the floor.

RHYTHM AND SEQUENCING: LISTENING TO THE BEAT
Musical Instruments

Use different musical instruments to beat out a rhythm:

- ❏ tambourine
- ❏ maracas
- ❏ tulip block
- ❏ wood block
- ❏ chime bars
- ❏ metal or wooden chime bars
- ❏ glockenspiel
- ❏ piano
- ❏ drum

Homemade musical instruments

- ❏ empty biscuit tin and a wooden spoon
- ❏ upturned box or bucket and a stick
- ❏ two shells to tap together
- ❏ two sticks to tap together

RHYTHM AND SEQUENCING: LISTENING TO LONG AND SHORT
Teaching Activity

'Colour My Chart'

You will need:
a recorder; marker pens:
several pieces of paper with drawings of long and short rectangles.

Useful words and phrases:
look; listen; drum(s);
wait; long; short;
name of musical instrument.

What to do:

1. Explain to the child that you are going to play a listening game, and give her the piece of paper. You will be making some sounds. When she hears a long sound, she must colour in one of the long rectangles. If she hears a short sound, she must colour in one of the short rectangles.

2. Make a long sound and say to the child, "That was a long sound". Encourage her to colour in the long rectangle.

3. Make a short sound. Tell the child, "That was a short sound". Encourage her to colour in the short rectangle.

4. Next see if the child can colour in the rectangle without any help.

5. If she fails to make a response, repeat the sound. If she still has difficulty, tell the child whether the sound was long or short. Repeat it and help her colour in the appropriate rectangles.

To increase the complexity of the activity
- reduce the difference between the long and short sound;
- use a quieter sound;
- introduce a delay before the child is allowed to respond.

Variations
- Vary the sounds.
- Use different shapes or patterns.
- Use the coloured patterns for book covers or pictures.

RHYTHM AND SEQUENCING: LISTENING TO LONG AND SHORT
Activities for Early Years Settings

These activities give the children experience of listening to long and short sounds in musical instruments. Let them watch first and then try the activities with listening alone. Use one sound maker for each activity.

☐ Movement to long and short sounds

Show the children how to make a movement when you make a sound on a musical instrument. This could be raising their arms above their heads. Explain to the children that you are going to make the sound longer. They must raise their arms and slowly lower them to the side until the sound stops. Alternate between long and short sounds so the children can see and feel the different movements. (Try using a recorder, flute, or whistle.)

☐ Long and short lotto games

Two or three children can play this game. Make lotto cards that have six boxes. Draw either a long rectangle or a short rectangle in each of the boxes. Make each card different, so that some children have more long shapes and some more short. You will also need several counters. When the child hears a long sound, she must place her counter on a long rectangle. When she hears a short sound, she must place a counter on a short rectangle. Vary your presentation of the sounds: for example, two long sounds then a short sound. The winner is the first child to complete her card. (Try making sounds with a whistle, recorder or flute.)

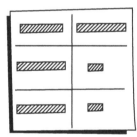

☐ Colour my chart

Draw on a piece of paper a long rectangle and next to this a short rectangle. (See illustration.) Repeat this pattern across the page. Explain to the child that you are going to play a listening game, and give her the piece of paper and some crayons. You will be making some sounds. When she hears a long sound, she must colour in one of the long rectangles. If she hears a short sound, she must colour in one of the short rectangles.

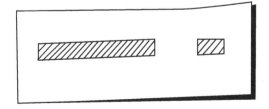

RHYTHM AND SEQUENCING: LISTENING TO LONG AND SHORT
Activities for Home

These activities give your child experience of listening to long and short sounds using musical instruments. Some of the games encourage her to copy the sounds. Use one sound maker for each activity.

☐ *Long and short*

Play some musical instruments that will help your child understand long and short. *Show* her long and short sounds on a party horn. Let her *feel* the vibrations with a mouth organ. Watch the little figure in a music box *move* with the music.

☐ *Recorder play*

Ask your child to draw a line on a long piece of paper (try an old roll of wallpaper) when you play a note on a recorder. She must stop drawing when the sound stops. Make lots of long and short sounds. Your child can look at the patterns she has drawn at the end.

☐ *Station master!*

Your child will have fun playing the station master in this game. You will need a toy train and a whistle. (Check that the sound of the whistle is not too piercing before you start.) Explain to your child that the train can only move when the station master is blowing his whistle. Give your child the train and blow your whistle. Vary between short and long blows on the whistle, making sure your child stops the train when the whistle stops. Let her have a turn at making sounds for you to push the train. (Dress up in a cap and wave a red flag!)

RHYTHM AND SEQUENCING: LISTENING TO LONG AND SHORT
Musical Instruments

The following musical instruments can be used for long and short listening games:

- ☐ whistle
- ☐ recorder
- ☐ flute
- ☐ horn
- ☐ party horn
- ☐ mouth organ

RHYTHM AND SEQUENCING: LISTENING TO FAST AND SLOW
Teaching Activity

'Parking the Car'

You will need:
a floor layout of streets; small model cars;
a drum with a beater; a screen.

Useful words and phrases:
look; listen; car; parking;
traffic jam; street or road;
wait; fast; slow.

What to do:

1 Introduce the drum to the child. Beat the drum slowly. Then beat the drum quickly. (Be careful to keep the volume the same when you change the rate of beating.)

2 Explain to the child that the cars need to be parked. Show her a parking space on the layout. When the drum is beaten quickly the cars can drive fast, but when the drum is beaten slowly the cars are crawling along in a traffic jam.

3 Place a car on a road on the layout. Let the child watch and listen to the drum before moving the car.

4 When she is consistent at responding appropriately to the drum, try a purely auditory activity. Place the drum out of sight behind a screen and repeat the activity. If the child is having difficulty, repeat the sound and, if necessary, let her see you make the sound.

5 Continue until all the cars have been parked.

To increase the complexity of the activity
- use fewer repetitions of the sound;
- reduce the difference between a fast and slow beat;
- introduce a delay before the child is allowed to respond.

Variations
- Let the child beat the drum.
- Use different model vehicles, such as fire engines, police cars and ambulances.
- Instead of cars on roads, use trains on railway lines; aeroplanes taking off and landing at airports; animals moving into a field or Noah's Ark; miniature dolls running or walking slowly along the pavement.

RHYTHM AND SEQUENCING: LISTENING TO FAST AND SLOW

Activities for Early Years Settings

These activities help the children to practise their skills in discriminating fast and slow rhythms in musical instruments. Vary the instruments you use but make sure you only use one instrument in each game. If the instruments are different, the children may be responding to the different sounds and not a difference in pace.

❏ *Dance to the beat*

Encourage the children to move in time with the beat of a song or piece of music. Help the children by beating out the rhythm on a drum. They can clap along with the rhythm.

❏ *Change the rhythm*

Use wood blocks to play this game. Create different rhythmic patterns by using a combination of quick and slow beats. More able children can mark the beats onto a card. Each beat can be represented by a dot. A fast rhythm might have the dots closer together and vice versa for a slow rhythm. Write out a pattern on a card for the child to copy.

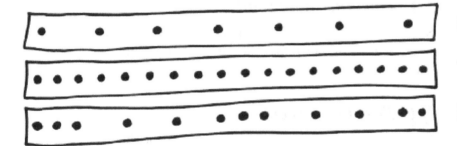

slow beat
fast beat
mixed beat

❏ *Do the funky caterpillar*

This game is great fun even if you do get a dirty bottom! Tell the children to sit on the floor in a long line with their legs outstretched. Each child should be sitting between the legs of the child behind. Explain that they are a caterpillar. They must grasp the ankle of the child behind with the left hand, and wave the right hand in the air. The children must shuffle along the floor like a caterpillar to the beat of a drum. When the rhythm changes from fast to slow or slow to fast, the children must change direction. (The rocking movement and waving arms look most effective!) Two caterpillars can have a race or one line has to catch up with the other.

Copyright material from Diana Williams (2020), *Early Listening Skills for Children with a Hearing Loss*, Second Edition, Routledge

RHYTHM AND SEQUENCING: LISTENING TO FAST AND SLOW
Activities for Home

These activities will help your child in listening for fast and slow rhythms in music and musical instruments. For musical instrument games, only use one so your child is listening to a change in pace and not a change in instrument.

☐ *Dancing*

Play music that has different beats for your child. Encourage her to dance quickly to fast music and slowly to music with a gentle beat. Quick steps could be skipping, hopping, side steps; slow steps could be knee bends, twirls on tip-toe and long strides.

☐ *Fast beat*

Experiment with making sounds at different speeds. Use a drum or a stick with an upturned bucket. Play some slow beats: da---da---da, then some quick beats: da-da-da. Can your child copy the rhythm? (Do not worry if the rhythm is not exactly the same speed. Your child should be aiming just to make a difference between fast and slow.)

☐ *Hoisting up the sails*

Show your child how to 'hoist up the sails'. She should speed up for a fast beat and slow down for a slow beat. Beat out a rhythm for her on a tambourine or a triangle.

☐ *Pass the parcel*

Play this version of 'pass the parcel' at a party. The children pass a parcel around a circle in time to the ring of a bell. When the bell is rung quickly, they must change direction and pass the parcel the other way. When the bell stops ringing, one wrapper of the parcel is opened. Continue with the game until all the layers are removed. The child who removes the last layer gets to keep the gift inside.

RHYTHM AND SEQUENCING: LISTENING TO FAST AND SLOW
Musical Instruments

A variety of musical instruments or sound makers can be used for fast or slow rhythms:

- ☐ drum
- ☐ triangle
- ☐ chime bars
- ☐ tambourine
- ☐ hand-held bell
- ☐ guitar
- ☐ wood blocks and mallet

Homemade musical instruments

- ☐ empty biscuit tin and a wooden spoon
- ☐ frying pan with a wooden spoon
- ☐ two sticks to tap together
- ☐ plastic flower pot and a stick to tap together
- ☐ two saucepans lids to bang together

RHYTHM AND SEQUENCING
Generalization of Rhythm Skills

Here are some suggestions for ways the child can generalize the skills she has learnt.

- Show the child how to use both hands to beat out a rhythm.
- Give the child practice at recalling rhythms by listening alone.
- Show her how to use different parts of her body to beat out a rhythm, such as tapping her foot, clapping, stamping, drumming fingers, banging and knocking with her hand.
- Try clapping games, action songs and rhymes that integrate a number of different rhythmic features. Examples include 'Pat-a-Cake' and other clapping games; skipping games; action songs, such as 'Wind the Bobbin up'; finger rhymes, such as 'Two Little Dickie Birds Sitting on a Wall'.
- Use musical instruments so that two hands are beating out the rhythm: for example, holding two maracas, banging two cymbals together or clicking castanets in each hand.
- Try listening to and dancing along to Scottish, tap, square and flamenco music, which all have a strong beat.

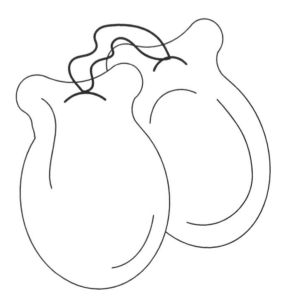

RHYTHM AND SEQUENCING: SEQUENCING SOUNDS
Teaching Activity

'One, Two . . . '

You will need:
two identical pairs of musical instruments – two drums, two bells; a screen.

Useful words and phrases:
listen; look; wait; first; second; one; two; copy; drum; bells.

What to do:

1. Check that the child is able to identify an instrument by sound alone.

2. Introduce the instruments to the child. Allow her some time to play with them and explore making some sounds.

3. Explain that you are going to play a listening game. Place one set of instruments in front of her within easy reach.

4. Seat yourself opposite the child with your matching instruments.

5. Tell her you are going to make two sounds. Ask her to watch and listen. Make a sound with one of your instruments. Explain that this is the first sound. Encourage her to copy you with her own instrument.

6. Make a sound with the other instrument. Explain that this is the second sound. Encourage her to copy you with her own instrument.

7. Repeat steps five and six, but this time ask the child to wait until you have finished before she plays her instruments.

8. Encourage her to play the sounds in the same order as you.

9. Make sure that the child is confident at sequencing the two sounds by watching and listening before trying a purely auditory task.

Section 7: Rhythm and Sequencing

10 Hide your set of instruments behind a screen. Tell the child that you are going to make the first sound and then play that sound for several seconds. (Keep the child's attention focused on you so that she is ready to attend to the second sound.) Now tell her that you are going to make the second sound. Make the second sound for several seconds. Ask her to make the same two sounds as you.

11 If she has difficulty, repeat the sounds. If she continues to be unsure, ask her to copy the sounds one at a time. Then repeat both sounds for her to copy.

To increase the complexity of the activity

- increase the number of sounds to be sequenced;
- use musical instruments that sound increasingly similar;
- use fewer repetitions of the sound;
- use less familiar musical instruments;
- introduce a delay before the child is allowed to respond.

Variations

- Use different musical instruments.
- Ask the child to point to pictures of the instruments.

RHYTHM AND SEQUENCING: SEQUENCING SOUNDS
Activities for Early Years Settings

These games will help the child to learn about sequencing sounds from musical instruments. You will need to have duplicate sets of instruments for the child to copy the sequences. Some activities can be carried out with small groups of children.

❑ *Finish the sequence*

Get ready three musical instruments with matching pictures. Draw two large squares on a piece of card. Place one of the pictures on the first square. Place the other two pictures of musical instruments in view. Behind a screen, make the sound of the musical instrument in the picture on the first square. Play the sound of another instrument. The child has to complete the sequence by choosing one of the two pictures. Gradually increase the number of pictures the child has to sequence.

❑ *Pass the sound*

This simple game can be played with a group of children using a musical instrument like a tambourine. Each child takes a turn to pass the tambourine round the circle to make a sound. Add another instrument. The children take it in turns to play two sounds in the correct sequence.

❑ *Follow the leader*

You will need two or three pairs of matching musical instruments. Divide the pairs of instruments among a group of children. Two or three children each make a sound for the other children to copy in the same order. Can the children copy the sequence of sounds if the other children play their instruments out of sight?

❑ *Sequencing shakers*

You will need two sets of shakers, such as two beakers with some bricks and two wooden boxes filled with pencils. Place one set in view of the children. Use the other set to play a sequence of two sounds. Choose a child to copy the sequence using the duplicate set. Put the objects behind a screen. Can the children copy the sequence by listening alone? Gradually increase the number of object sounds to be sequenced.

❑ *Volume and pitch*

Use different objects in the containers so that volume and pitch can be varied: for example, rice will sound different from wooden bricks. Or use different containers for the same objects: for example, a brick shaken in a tin will sound very different from one shaken in a plastic tub.

RHYTHM AND SEQUENCING: SEQUENCING SOUNDS
Activities for Home

Here are some ways of introducing the idea of sequences of sound to your child.

☐ *Everyday sequences*

Draw your child's attention to the sequence of sounds in everyday activities. For example, washing has the sounds of running water, splashing, the plug being pulled in the basin. Other sequences are: having breakfast – cereal shaken from the packet, milk poured into the bowl, spooning up the food; bath time – putting in the plug, running the water, pouring in bubble bath and swishing the water. Can you think of sequences of sounds that you hear every day?

☐ *Sounds on a walk*

Draw your child's attention to the sounds you hear on a walk to the shops or the nursery. Do you always hear the same sounds in the same order? Talk to your child about them. Show her how the order changes when you walk back or go a different way.

☐ *Copy a sequence*

You will need a couple of musical instruments or everyday items that make a sound (these could be a couple of bricks in a box or stirring a spoon in a cup). Make sure you and your child both have a set of sound makers. Show your child how you can make a sound with each instrument or object. Encourage her to copy you using her own sound makers. At first, she may need to make sounds along with you. Later, you can make the sounds out of sight. Can she copy the sequence by listening alone?

RHYTHM AND SEQUENCING: SEQUENCING SOUNDS
Musical Instruments

Try using a variety of musical instruments and shakers for sequencing games:

- ☐ jingle bells
- ☐ triangles
- ☐ tone blocks
- ☐ tambourines
- ☐ cabasa afuche
- ☐ tulip block
- ☐ jingle stick
- ☐ drum
- ☐ shakers

RHYTHM AND SEQUENCING
Record Sheet

Child's name	

Date	Activity	Observations
Example 1.3.	*Game of 'Mark a pattern'. Barrier game with one other child. Using a drum. (AI)*	*Making dots with a paint marker. Able to make a mark after the drum beat. Very careful with her mark making, and was missing some beats.*

AI = adult initiated activity; CI = child initiated activity

SECTION 8
Auditory Memory

Introduction *149*

Factors Affecting the Child's Auditory
Memory *150*

Teaching Guidance *152*

Strategies *155*

    Activities for Early Years Settings *157*

    Activities for Home *160*

Record Sheet *162*

INTRODUCTION

Auditory memory is an important and integral part of listening, language and communication skills. The child needs to attend to, process, store and retrieve information if she is to recognize and use sounds and speech in a meaningful way. Some children have difficulties with auditory memory, and this is often the case for children with a hearing loss. These activities would also benefit other children who need to develop their attention, concentration and listening skills.

All listening activities involve memory to a certain extent, although different activities will have more or less of a memory load for the child. Advice is provided in this section on how to modify tasks to increase or decrease the memory load for the child. Factors affecting the child's ability to remember auditory stimuli are also outlined, with specific guidance on how to choose auditory stimuli and the use of appropriate language.

Activities for building auditory memory are provided, with suggestions for how to model and encourage the development of memory strategies. The section on 'Listening to Spoken Language', in conjunction with the guidance in this section, can also be used to work on auditory memory.

AUDITORY MEMORY
Factors Affecting the Child's Auditory Memory

The child's ability to remember auditory stimuli will be affected by the factors in the following list, some of which relate to the child and others to the nature of the task presented to the child.

- *The child's hearing* – a child with a hearing loss is likely to have difficulty with auditory memory.
- *The child's health and well-being* – a child who is tired, unwell or otherwise not comfortable will find it difficult to concentrate.
- *The child's language level* – a lack of language skills may make extra demands on the child's ability to complete an activity, thus affecting her memory capacity.
- *The child's familiarity with the adult* – the child may become withdrawn or 'play up' when with an unfamiliar adult.
- *Formal or informal situations* – it may be harder for the child to remember under the pressure of a situation where she is being tested. On the contrary, the child may be too relaxed in an informal atmosphere and be less inclined to concentrate.
- *Time pressures* – is there a time limit on the activity? Is it near dinnertime? Is the child competing with another child? All these pressures may have an adverse effect on the child's ability to remember.
- *The age of the child* – memory skills are linked with language and develop with age.
- *The cognitive abilities of the child* – memory skills are linked with the cognitive level of the child.
- *A noisy background* – the child will be distracted and find it harder to listen with competing auditory stimuli.
- *A busy visual background* – the child will be distracted and find it hard to concentrate with competing stimuli.

Memory loading (or level of cognitive demand) can be increased by all of the following:

- new activities;
- unfamiliar materials;
- the amount of language the child is required to understand during the activity;
- a task involving several skills rather than one skill;

Section 8: Auditory Memory

- multi-tasking;
- auditory stimuli that are very similar;
- complex auditory stimuli;
- the number of auditory stimuli the child has to choose between;
- a long delay before the child can respond;
- introducing a distraction before the child is allowed to recall items;
- the level of listening skill: for example, sound detection is easier than sound recognition;
- the number of items the child has to remember;
- asking the child to recall a sequence;
- the length of the activity.

AUDITORY MEMORY
Teaching Guidance

It is important to scaffold learning for children who have difficulty with auditory memory. Plan activities using the following guidelines, which show how to control memory load in activities, and indicate the steps for building auditory memory.

Get the child's attention
Make sure you are close to her and on her eye level. Call her name before giving an instruction.

Make language functional
Avoid asking the child to repeat lists without a context. Instead, make language *functional* by relating it to a task or communicative situation. So remembering items for a recipe or the names of children in a game.

Use familiar words and phrases
This means the activity is focused on memory and stops it from becoming a vocabulary or language comprehension task.

Use clear language

Keep language *simple* – use short sentences with simple sentence structures.

Be *specific* – avoid unclear or vague references; compare "put some musical instruments over there" with "put the drum and bell on the table".

Be *clear* – take out any unnecessary words or phrases: for example, avoid a tag question at the end of a sentence: "Find me your socks and shoes, *will you*?"

Use *chunking* – break instructions down into smaller chunks of information. Pause between them to give the child time to process and recall items.

Sequence instructions clearly – give instructions in the order you want them carried out.

Section 8: Auditory Memory

Emphasize key words – use acoustic highlighting to emphasize important words by saying them louder and longer. (Make sure you maintain your normal intonation patterns and avoid distorting speech sounds.)

Use *repetition* – repeat the whole phrase, not just the key words or elements, or the key words or elements the child has forgotten.

Use *redundancy* – use redundant language in an instruction, so the child can focus on the key words. For example, the words 'give me' become redundant if you hold out your hand as you give the request. This way the child still has the appropriate language modelled.

Build auditory memory

Auditory memory tasks need to gradually increase from the simple to more complex.

Start with one key word or critical element:

"Find the *drum*"

Gradually increase to two, three and more elements.

"Find the *drum* and *bells*"

"Find the *drum*, *bells* and *tambourine*"

Use phonologically dissimilar words:

pot, pan, pen ✘
pen, book, ruler ✓

And acoustically distinct sound makers:

maraca, cabasa afuche, egg shaker ✘
hand bell, maraca, drum ✓

Choose words that are easy to say:

scrunchie ✘
band ✓

Start with single syllable words and build to multi-syllable words:

butterfly, caterpillar ✘
bird, duck, dog ✓

Section 8: Auditory Memory

Use words in similar categories:

Start with items in the same category (for example, animals or clothes); or items from the same context (such as art materials or items for a backpack). Some activities intrinsically work on categories, so a shopping game will have related food items.

Use visual clues:

- Use visual props, for example, present items of food in a shopping memory game;
- Provide a visual indicator of the number of items the child has to recall, for example, two boxes for two selected objects;
- Use cue cards with pictures, signs, or text (if appropriate);
- Use physical prompts, gesture and sign.

AUDITORY MEMORY
Strategies

Encourage the child to develop strategies that help auditory memory by modelling techniques and incorporating them into activities.

☐ *Rehearsal*

Adults use vocal and subvocal rehearsal to help them remember things. Children can be encouraged to use a vocal rehearsal strategy by repeating lists, simple phrases and commands. You can help by:

- modelling vocal rehearsal in everyday situations;
- using turn taking in games as an opportunity to model vocal rehearsal;
- encouraging the child to repeat an instruction aloud before she carries out the request with prompts like, "Tell me what you heard";
- modelling quiet (or saying it to yourself) vocal rehearsal.

As children develop their skills with longer commands, you might try adding in a delay after you give an instruction to allow the child time to rehearse. Eventually children will be able to rehearse instructions quietly to themselves, and ultimately silently (subvocal rehearsal), but the latter is a much more complex skill expected of older children.

☐ *Visualization*

Visualizing or making a mental image of information that we have heard can help us to remember that information. Try to:

- encourage children to make a picture in their head of a word.
- combine visual and auditory memory tasks. This will help the child in building up the necessary visual information alongside the auditory information.
- use sensory integration through exploration and discussion of what the different senses can tell us about an object. For example, an apple is round, green, hard, sweet to taste and has a distinct smell.

☐ *Making links*

Help children to make connections between items they want to remember by:

- presenting items in a task from the same semantic category;
- playing category and association games to help build up knowledge of these connections;
- modelling how to use associations to help memory, for example, saying out loud "I need to buy some *fruit*, . . . banana, apple and pear".

Section 8: Auditory Memory

☐ *Targeting*

Identifying the key word or main idea is an essential sub skill in memory tasks. Instead of trying to recall unimportant details, the child needs to focus on (or target) their attention on the most relevant parts of the message. Use strategies like:

- acoustic highlighting of key words;
- pausing before and after saying something important;
- repetition of the key points.

AUDITORY MEMORY: STRATEGIES
Activities for Early Years Settings

Here are some activities using sounds, words and simple phrases that help build auditory memory and provide opportunities to model and practice memory strategies.

☐ *'Simon says'*

Play 'Simon says'. Ask the child to do an action: "Simon says clap your hands". At first, 'say' and 'do' the action with the child; later, just give a verbal instruction. Gradually make the commands longer by adding two, or three different actions: "Simon says clap your hands and touch your toes". Encourage the child to do the actions in the correct sequence. Let the child have a turn at giving you instructions. Show the child how to use repetition or rehearsal of the instruction to help memory.

☐ *Name game*

There are various name games to suit different age groups:

- Roll, roll the ball (sung to the tune of 'Row, row, row your boat'*)

    - Sing "Roll, roll, roll the ball" (roll the ball to the child)
    - "Roll the ball to _____ (child's name)"
    - "_____ _____ _____ _____" (Repeat the child's name)
    - "Roll the ball to _____" (use your name)

*Original verse:

Row, row, row your boat

Gently down the stream,

Merrily, merrily, merrily, merrily

Life is but a dream

Let each child have a turn at singing and rolling the ball.

- Bean bag

Children throw a beanbag to each other, but before they throw the bag they must name the catcher.

- Get to know you

Play this game with a small group of children. Each child says their name, and something they like, such as, "I am Asha, I like cake". The

Section 8: Auditory Memory

next person must repeat what the previous child has said and then add their own name and what they like. For example, "Asha likes cake. I am Yanni, and I like playing football". And so on until they get round the group. Allow children to prompt if someone forgets a name or some information. You could follow up by asking questions like, "Who liked cake?'

📋 *Barrier games*

Play this listening game with children who can follow simple instructions involving familiar language. You will need to place a barrier between you and the child. This can be made of anything, but should allow the child to see your face. You will need identical sets of equipment, for example, miniature items of furniture, people and animals. Set up a scene with your toys – the cat on the bed, the chair on the table. Give instructions to the child on how to set up her scene. There are lots of opportunities to repeat instructions by both the adult and the child. Once the child is ready you can remove the barrier and compare scenes.

Other ideas include:

- Dressing cut out characters in different clothing
- Drawings or colouring in pictures
- Following colour patterns with bricks or counters

📋 *Pelmanism*

Pelmanism or a pairs game involves having several matching pairs of pictures that are turned over and mixed up. Each player takes turns to turn over two cards to find a match. Encourage the child to name all the items at the beginning of the game, and name the pictures again when she turns over a pair. Even though it is a visual memory game, she will be able to think of the word to help remember the picture. It will also help her practice rehearsal and repetition strategies.

This game can be easily adapted to make it auditory only. For example, instead of turning a picture over, the player takes a peek and says, "I found a cat", and then puts it back down where the other player cannot see it. Players then have to use their auditory memory, holding that information in their head while remembering what the other person saw.

📋 *Stories*

Follow up listening to a picture storybook by asking the child questions about key information. Can they recall the characters and something about the plot? For example, in 'Goldilocks', you might ask questions about what were the bears eating? What was wrong with daddy's porridge? Where was Goldilocks when the bears found her? Why was Goldilocks sleeping in baby bear's bed? Can she re-tell the story in her own words? Provide some toy material to help her act out the key points of the story.

Section 8: Auditory Memory

☐ *Simon game (online)*

This is an online version of the electronic game 'Simon' with the traditional four coloured keys of red, blue, yellow and green. These keys are randomly lit in various degrees of difficulty, from one colour, to two colours and as many as the player can manage to remember. As in the original game, the aim is to repeat the pattern by clicking on the same colour keys. Help the child to understand and process the information she is seeing by saying the names of the colours out loud as they light up, "red, yellow" or "red, red, blue". (We often process visual information in an auditory way like this. Think about when we read, we see letters but think of sounds.) Encourage her to say the sequence aloud again as she tries to repeat the sequence.

Available on desktops, smartphones and tablets with free and unlimited download at: www.memozor.com/other-free-memory-games-online/simon-games/simon-game

AUDITORY MEMORY: STRATEGIES
Activities for Home

Here are some activities using sounds, words and simple phrases that help build auditory memory and provide opportunities to model and practice memory strategies.

☐ *At the supermarket*

Ask your child to find items as you shop at the supermarket. Choose items in a similar group, so one or two vegetables or fruits. Encourage your child to make a picture in her head of the foods or objects you name. Tell your child you are going to ask for some 'vegetables' or 'biscuits' or 'drinks'. Gradually increase the number of items. Some supermarkets have a mini trolley for children, so your child can collect her 'shopping', and see how much she has remembered.

☐ *Word games*

Word games are based around remembering a list of words, so you will need two or three children or adults to play the game. The word game 'I went shopping and bought . . .' can follow on from the previous activity.

At first, you can have toys or objects to act as prompts. So, for example, one person starts by choosing an item from a shopping bag, and says, "I went shopping and bought an apple". The next person must repeat the phrase and the name of the item, then take a new item from the bag to add to the list. They must repeat the phrase with the two items of food – "I went shopping and bought an apple and some beans."

Gradually remove the props and encourage your child to listen to the words. Help her to remember the sequence too. To make a more fun activity, use items for a recipe that you then make together with your child.

Other scenarios might include:
I went to the zoo and saw . . .
I went on holiday and took . . .
I went to . . . and saw . . .

☐ *Go and ask . . .*

Ask your child to follow a simple request, for example, "Go and ask Tina for some paper and a crayon". Encourage your child to repeat the request before she follows the instruction. You can say the repetition along with her. Relate the requests to an activity: for example, ingredients for a recipe, or clothing and toys for a visit to the park. At the end, use repetition again by checking you have all the items you need.

Section 8: Auditory Memory

☐ *Nursery rhymes and action songs*

Learn a well-known rhyme or a song you can sing with your child and do actions together. For example, 'Wheels on the Bus' has lots of fun actions that use hands, arms and whole body movements. Good rhymes with finger play are 'Twinkle, Twinkle Little Star' and 'Itsy-bitsy Spider'.

Leave pauses for your child to fill in the words or phrases. Start with the last word in a phrase and build up to a sentence: for example, "Round and round the Mulberry . . . (bush)".

☐ *Story rhyme picture books*

Read picture storybooks that have repetitive rhymes your child can join in repeating: for example, 'In the Dark, Dark Wood' by Jessica Souhami or 'Funnybones' by Janet and Allan Ahlberg.

☐ *Add a line*

Use a page from a magazine or a catalogue. Give your child some coloured pens and ask her to make different lines: for example, "Draw a cross on the hat" and "Draw a line under the chair". Let her choose her favourite colours to make the lines.

☐ *Treasure hunt*

Hide fun items like a squeaky toy, a lift the flap book or some bubbles around the home. Give your child instructions, e.g., "walk to the kitchen", "check under the dish". You can start with short, simple instructions, and make the instructions longer as your child is able to follow more complex commands. You can have fun at the end playing with your treasure trove.

AUDITORY MEMORY
Record Sheet

Child's name	

Date	Activity/Context	Observations
Example 22.5.	*Playing 'I went shopping' game with two other children and teacher. (AI)*	*Remembered two items without help. Used verbal rehearsal when prompted. This helped her to remember three items.*

AI = adult initiated activity; CI = child initiated activity

SECTION 9
Listening to Spoken Language

Introduction	*165*
Listening To Single Words	*166*
Food	*167*
Teaching Activity	*167*
Activities for Early Years Settings	*169*
Activities for Home	*170*
Materials and Equipment	*171*
Clothes	*172*
Teaching Activity	*172*
Activities for Early Years Settings	*173*
Activities for Home	*175*
Materials and Equipment	*176*
Body Parts	*177*
Teaching Activity	*177*

Activities for Early Years Settings 178

Activities for Home 179

Materials and Equipment.. 180

Animals 181

Teaching Activity 181

Activities for Early Years Settings 182

Activities for Home 183

Materials and Equipment.. 184

Action Words... 185

Teaching Activity 185

Activities for Early Years Settings 186

Activities for Home 187

Materials and Equipment.. 188

Listening To Simple Commands 189

Listening To Complex Commands 191

Record Sheet.. 193

INTRODUCTION

A *child* develops spoken language through listening to speech and learning to imitate what she hears. Through a variety of experiences, sound becomes meaningful to her and eventually she understands that a word represents an object, an event, a feeling or a person. Not only is she aware of speech, but she is also able to attach meaning to it. However, even at this stage of development, there are some children who find it difficult to listen to spoken language, even though they understand the words.

The activities in this section are designed to help those children who understand spoken language but who have difficulty in maintaining attention to speech. They are particularly relevant for children with a fluctuating hearing loss (or glue ear), but are also useful for helping attention and concentration skills in general. The games involve single words, simple commands and complex instructions. These are not activities for language teaching, although children's communication will be enhanced by any group activity involving interaction.

As the activities are designed to develop listening skills and not comprehension of speech, the vocabulary should be familiar to the child. You can check the child's understanding by asking her to name the items before you start the game. Some children may need you to use a gesture or sign along with the spoken command, or additional cues like a symbol or picture card showing the item.

In general, children should start at the single-word level and build up to longer and more complex instructions. Remember that increasing the length and complexity of a command will increase the memory load for the child. Additional guidance on 'Auditory Memory' is provided in Section 8.

LISTENING TO SPOKEN LANGUAGE
Listening to Single Words

The following games are based on the idea of 'information carrying words' originally used by Knowles and Masidlover (1978) as the basis for the *Derbyshire Language Scheme* (www.derbyshire-language-scheme.co.uk*)*. The number of information carrying words (sometimes referred to as the key words or critical elements) will affect the complexity of a sentence.

You will not be able to find the number of information carrying words by simply counting the words in a sentence, as the words give only part of the message. The child uses other information from the situation, such as gestural cues and what she has learnt from the past, to help her to make sense of speech.

Some words in a sentence are redundant – they add nothing to the message. For example, the adult who says, "Give me the *ball*" while holding out her hand, is only requiring the child to understand 'ball'. The outstretched hand indicates to the child that the adult wants to be given something. This sentence, used in this context, will have one information carrying word. If there is no other toy in the immediate vicinity of the child, then 'ball' becomes redundant too. The child is likely to respond appropriately to the request even when she has not understood the verbal message.

Activities where the child is required to make a choice are likely to have information carrying words. So if you ask the child for a banana, there must be the choice between the banana and another item. Key words for listening practice can be used alone or placed in a simple sentence where the other words are redundant. The following games require the child to understand one information carrying word in the sentence.

Use the following groups of naming words for listening to single words:

- ❏ everyday objects
- ❏ food
- ❏ clothes
- ❏ animals
- ❏ body parts
- ❏ transport
- ❏ action words, such as run, walk, sit, jump
- ❏ prepositions

LISTENING TO SPOKEN LANGUAGE
LISTENING TO SINGLE WORDS: FOOD
Teaching Activity

'Let's Go Shopping'

You will need:
a shopping bag; a variety of replica food; a table or other surface that can be used as a 'pretend' shop counter.

Useful words and phrases:
look; listen; names of food; shopping; shop; bag.

What to do:

1. Explain to the child that you are going to play a shopping game. Bring out each item of food for her to name.

2. Discard any she is unable to name, and place the remaining food on a table. The items should be spaced out so that each item is clearly visible.

3. Make it clear to the child that this is a 'pretend' shop.

4. Tell the child that you are going to play shops. Give her a shopping bag and ask her to fetch an item from the shop: for example, "Buy an *apple*".

5. If the child is unsure, repeat the question or use a simpler request, such as "*apple*". It may be necessary to point to the item or make a gesture, such as pretending to take a bite from an apple, or use a picture cue. (Remember to continue to use sign if this is the child's preferred communication method.)

6. Ask the child to tell you what she has bought on her return with the bag.

7. Continue with the game until she has bought several items.

8. Can the child ask you to fetch some items?

To increase the complexity of the activity

- gradually increase the number of items the child has to choose between (maximum five to six);
- introduce a delay before the child is allowed to respond.

Variations

- Place mats on the floor as an imaginary path for the child to follow. This will add a natural delay before she is able to respond.
- Use real items of food, but be aware of any possible allergens!
- Use different groups or categories of food, like vegetables; dairy products; fruit; or drinks.
- Use food associated with special occasions such as festivals and religious events.

 Empty food and drink containers may contain traces of allergens: for example, cereal and biscuit boxes may contain traces of nut. Avoid egg cartons, milk cartons, cereal boxes, biscuit boxes and baby food jars.

LISTENING TO SPOKEN LANGUAGE
LISTENING TO SINGLE WORDS: FOOD
Activities for Early Years Settings

These games will help children with their listening skills. Although they will help communication skills, they are not designed specifically to teach language. It is expected that the children will know the vocabulary used in the listening activities.

❑ *Puzzles and jigsaws*
Some puzzles and jigsaws have pictures of single food items. The child can be asked to take out and put back pieces that you name.

❑ *Doll play*
Ask the child for food items at a doll's tea party or during play in the home corner.

❑ *Post it*
Place on a table several large photographs of food. Ask the child to find pictures of different foods. They can post the correct one into a box.

❑ *Matching pictures to food*
You will need several photographs or pictures of food with real items to match. Name different food items for the child to find and match to the pictures or photographs. Choose items that might be classified as in one category: for example, fruits, snacks, drinks or vegetables.

❑ *Restaurant*
Have a 'pretend' restaurant where one child is a waiter and the other children are the customers. The waiter must listen to the order from the children, which she then tells to you – the chef. (Make a picture menu – see illustration.)

❑ *My food eBook*
Use a Book Creator app on an android tablet or an iPad to make a digital book with the children about different foods. Ask children to share a favourite food from home for a taster activity. This is a great way for children to learn about food from different countries. Fruits and vegetables would be ideal for a single word activity. Take pictures of single items, and add these to the book. For EAL learners, the names of food spoken in their first language can be recorded.

LISTENING TO SPOKEN LANGUAGE
LISTENING TO SINGLE WORDS: FOOD
Activities for Home

These are games to help your child listen to names of food. For listening activities, it is important to use only food that your child knows and can also name. Check her understanding of words by asking her to name the items of food before you use them in the games.

❑ 'Pretend' shops

Use tins and other food items from the kitchen to play 'pretend' shops. Set up a shop on the table or floor. Give your child a shopping bag and ask her to fetch one item at a time for you: for example, say, "Buy a banana". Let your child send you to the shops. She must tell you what items to buy.

❑ Magazines

Look through magazines with your child and talk about your favourite food. Ask her to find the pictures of different food: for example, "Where's the cake?" This could be her favourite food, something she had for dinner or an ingredient for a recipe. Help her cut pictures out to make scrapbooks or collages.

❑ Teddy's picnic

Have a pretend picnic for your child's teddies. Your child can help you set out the picnic. Ask for different items, food and drink: for example, "let's lay out the picnic", "We need *cups*", "Where are the *apples*?" Take turns in the picnic to ask each other for food and drink for the teddies.

❑ Shopping

Your child can help you unpack the shopping. Ask for one item at a time. Can she put it away in the "cupboard" or in the "drawer"?

❑ Cooking

Your child can help collect together the ingredients for a recipe or items for a meal. She can help you cook it by doing simple tasks like washing vegetables, pouring flour, mixing ingredients or adding cheese to pizza.

LISTENING TO SPOKEN LANGUAGE
LISTENING TO SINGLE WORDS: FOOD

Materials and Equipment

Suggestions for toys and items that can be used to represent food are the following:

- ☐ real food
- ☐ life-sized replica food
- ☐ empty food containers!
- ☐ papier-mâché models
- ☐ pictures from magazines
- ☐ picture cards of single items of food
- ☐ photo cards of single items of food
- ☐ line drawings of single items of food

Empty real food and drink containers may contain traces of allergens, for example, cereal and biscuit boxes may contain traces of nut. Avoid egg cartons, milk cartons, cereal boxes, biscuit boxes and baby food jars.

LISTENING TO SPOKEN LANGUAGE
LISTENING TO SINGLE WORDS: CLOTHES
Teaching Activity

'Teddy is off on Holiday'

You will need:
a teddy; a small toy suitcase; doll-size clothes.

Useful words and phrases:
look; listen; names of clothing; suitcase; teddy; holiday.

What to do:

1. Explain to the child that teddy is going on holiday and he needs some help with packing his suitcase.

2. Bring out each item of clothing for the child to name. Discard any she is unable to name, and place the remaining items on the floor.

3. Lay the clothes out so that each item is clearly visible.

4. Ask the child to fetch an item of clothing: for example, "Where's teddy's *jumper*?"

5. If the child is unsure, repeat the question or use a simpler request, such as "*jumper*". It may be necessary to point to the item or make a gesture, such as pretending to pull a jumper over your head, or use a symbol or picture cue.

6. Ask the child to tell you what she has found before she packs it away in teddy's suitcase.

To increase the complexity of the activity

- gradually increase the number of items the child has to choose between (maximum five to six);
- introduce a delay before the child is allowed to respond.

Variations

- Instead of a suitcase, try a duffle bag; shoulder bag; cardboard box; basket; shoebox; sports bag; child's suitcase; or a pillowcase.
- Vary teddy's holiday destination: warm climate versus cold climate; beach holiday versus country holiday.
- Introduce other holiday items, such as sunglasses, sun hat, bucket and spade.

LISTENING TO SPOKEN LANGUAGE
LISTENING TO SINGLE WORDS: CLOTHES

Activities for Early Years Settings

These games will help children with their listening skills. Although they will help communication skills, they are not designed specifically to teach language. It is expected that the children will know the vocabulary used in the listening activities.

☐ *'Pretend' shop*

Set up a 'pretend' clothes shop using old clothes, baby or doll's clothes. Lay several items out on a table or other surface that can be used as a counter. You can play lots of games, including some listening activities. Shopkeeper: one child is the shopkeeper and the other children are the customers. The children take turns to ask for an item of clothing. The shopkeeper finds the item and makes a sale. Shopper: the children line up to go shopping. Each child is asked to buy one item for you.

☐ *Play 'Simon says get dressed'*

Play a dressing-up game using a version of 'Simon says'. Have lots of items of clothing, such as several hats, gloves, shoes, scarves and waistcoats. The children dress up in the items named by Simon - "Simon says put on your . . . *hat*". Children can take turns at being Simon and giving the instruction.

☐ *Team competition*

Divide the children into two teams. One child is chosen from each team to be the 'clothes horse'. Make sure there is a very large pile of clothes, such as hats, gloves, shoes, scarves and waistcoats for the children to sort through. The other children must dress their team member in the items of clothing you call out. The first team to finish dressing is the winner.

☐ *Doll play*

Play dressing-up games with a doll and some doll's clothes. Ask the child to dress the doll in the items as you name them.

Musical clothes

This is a version of musical chairs, but in this game the children must find an item of clothing to wear. You will need lots of clothes with several sets of the same item, such as hats or scarves. Before the start of the game, sort the clothes so that for the first turn of the game there should be enough items for all the children. For the second turn there should be one less than is needed, and so on until there is only one item of a particular piece of clothing: for example, five hats, four scarves, three pairs of gloves, two belts and one jacket. The children move around while you play some music. When the music stops you call out an item of clothing, such as "hat". The children must find a hat and put it on. The child who fails to find an item of clothing is out. Continue with the game and choose a different item of clothing next time. The last child 'in' is the winner.

Post it

Place several large photographs of clothes on a table with a posting box. Ask the child to find pictures of different clothes. They can post the correct one into a box.

Matching pictures to clothing

You will need several photographs or pictures of clothing with real items to match. Name different articles of clothing for the child to find and match to pictures or photographs. Choose clothes that are part of a theme: for example, sports clothes, school clothes, winter clothes, uniforms, clothes associated with different countries, cultures or festivals.

Washing line

Hang a washing line up in the room. Use real clothes, doll's clothes or cut-outs. Ask the children to hang up the clothes you name. Instructions could also be given by a puppet or doll: "Hang up my *coat*, please."

LISTENING TO SPOKEN LANGUAGE
LISTENING TO SINGLE WORDS: CLOTHES
Activities for Home

These games will help your child with her listening skills. For listening activities, it is important only to use clothes your child knows and can name. Check her understanding of words by asking her to name the items used in the games.

❏ *Fashion show*

Play at being a catwalk model with your child! Ask her to find different items of clothing for you to model. You can then do the same for her.

❏ *Magazines and clothes catalogues*

Look through magazines or a clothes catalogue with your child. Ask her to find pictures of different items of clothing. This could be her favourite party dress or a colourful swimsuit. If you are ordering clothes, maybe she could help you find the picture and reference number. Help her cut pictures out to make scrapbooks or collages.

❏ *Doll play*

Play dressing-up games with a doll and some doll's clothes. Ask your child to dress the doll in the items as you name them. You can use a real doll or put paper clothes on a cardboard cut-out figure.

❏ *Dressing*

When your child is dressing, ask her to fetch different clothes to put on. Avoid asking for the items in the order of dressing, otherwise she can guess what you want!

❏ *Laundry*

Ask your child to sort your laundry, saying, "Find the *socks*" and "Find the *towels*". Can she put away your ironing as you name the items?

LISTENING TO SPOKEN LANGUAGE
LISTENING TO SINGLE WORDS: CLOTHES

Materials and Equipment

Try using the following items in listening games with a clothes theme:

- ☐ real clothing
- ☐ baby clothes
- ☐ doll's clothing
- ☐ pictures from magazines and catalogues
- ☐ cardboard cut-outs
- ☐ paper dolls and cut-out clothes
- ☐ picture cards of single items of clothing
- ☐ photo cards of single items of clothing
- ☐ line drawings of single items of clothing

LISTENING TO SPOKEN LANGUAGE
LISTENING TO SINGLE WORDS: BODY PARTS

Teaching Activity

'Give Dolly a Bath'

You will need:

a large doll; a plastic baby bath filled with tepid water; a sponge; a bar of soap; a towel; an apron.

Useful words and phrases:

look; listen; names of body parts; wash; dry; bath; water; soap; sponge; towel.

What to do:

1. The child may need to wear an apron and roll her sleeves up, as this game involves water play.

2. Introduce the doll, washing items and bath to the child and explain that dolly needs a bath.

3. Show the child how to lather up the sponge with the soap. Talk to the child as you wash different parts of the doll: for example, "Now I'm washing dolly's *hands*".

4. Let the child have a turn, hand her the sponge and ask her to listen carefully. Tell her, "Wash dolly's *hands*".

5. If the child is unsure, repeat the instruction or use a simpler command, such as "Wash *hands*". It may be necessary to point to the doll's hands or make a gesture, such as showing her your hands.

6. Continue the activity, naming different parts of the body.

To increase the complexity of the activity

- gradually increase the number of body parts to wash: for example, "Wash dolly's *hands* and *feet*";
- introduce a delay before the child is allowed to respond.

Variations

- Use a teddy instead of a dolly.
- When you have finished bathing dolly, encourage the child to use the towel to dry parts of dolly as you name them: for example, "Dry dolly's *back*".

**LISTENING TO SPOKEN LANGUAGE
LISTENING TO SINGLE WORDS: BODY PARTS**

Activities for Early Years Settings

These games will help children with their listening skills. Although they will help communication skills, they are not designed specifically to teach language. It is expected that the children will know the vocabulary used in the listening activities.

☐ *Point to your ...*

Ask the child to point to body parts on herself or other children. Children can have fun by sticking gold stars on different body parts.

☐ *Bean bag rock*

Sing along with this song that uses bean bags to encourage children to make different actions and to place the bean bag on different body parts. Find this song and other bean bag activities on 'Bean Bag Activities and Coordination Skills' by Kimbo Georgiana Stewart. Available in several formats (CD, MP3 player, streaming).

☐ *Body parts lotto*

Ask the child to find pictures of body parts that you name and then match them to a picture lotto board. Suitable cards and lotto boards are available from commercial educational suppliers; however, there are many free down loadable resources online. Just search online with the term 'body parts lotto'.

☐ *Draw an outline*

Using large sheets of paper, ask the child to draw round different parts of her own body and parts of other children's bodies.

☐ *Find the picture*

Place several pictures or photographs of body parts on the table or floor. Ask the child, "Where is the *hand*?" and so on. Make the game more fun by turning the pictures face down.

☐ *Patchwork dolly*

Make a giant drawing of a doll or teddy, and cut it into different body parts. (Keep the face blank, and have pictures of eyes, a nose, a mouth and so on to stick on the face.) Ask the child for different body parts to put it back together again.

LISTENING TO SPOKEN LANGUAGE
LISTENING TO SINGLE WORDS: BODY PARTS
Activities for Home

These games will help your child with her listening skills. For listening activities it is important only to use body parts your child knows and can name. Check her understanding of words by playing the copying game (described next) first.

☐ Copying game

Point to your eyes as you name them. Encourage your child to copy you, and say "eyes". Point to your nose as you name it. Encourage your child to copy you, and say "nose". Repeat with as many body part names your child is able to name.

☐ Show me . . .

Ask your child to show you different body parts as you name them: for example, "Show me your *eyes*."

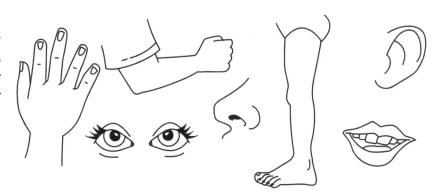

☐ Bath time

Ask your child to wash different body parts at bath time. (Change the order around each day.) Have a game with your child to see if she can guess which part is next. Dolly or teddy can have a bath too. Tell your child, "Wash dolly's *hair*" or "Wash dolly's *face*".

☐ Nursery rhymes and action songs

Nursery rhymes and action songs provide your child with repetitive phrases and words. Try stopping before the last word for your child to join in. Some are useful for teaching words on a particular theme, such as 'This is the way we wash our face; this is the way we comb our hair' (body parts and action words) or 'Heads, shoulders, knees and toes' (body parts).

☐ Picture books

Look at people in picture books. Can your child point to the different body parts as you name them?

LISTENING TO SPOKEN LANGUAGE
LISTENING TO SINGLE WORDS: BODY PARTS

Materials and Equipment

Try using the following items in games:

- ❏ pictures from magazines or catalogues
- ❏ picture cards
- ❏ photo cards
- ❏ line drawings
- ❏ papier-mâché models of body parts
- ❏ body parts on teddies and puppets
- ❏ body prints: for example, paint your hand and make a print
- ❏ shadows cast by body parts
- ❏ front, back and side views of body parts

LISTENING TO SPOKEN LANGUAGE
LISTENING TO SINGLE WORDS: ANIMALS
Teaching Activity

'Farmyard Animals'

You will need:
three small plastic animal shapes (for example, a cow, a duck and a horse);
a model farm.

Useful words and phrases:
look; listen; names of animals; farm; farmyard; farmer; escape; lost.

What to do:

1. Show the model farm to the child.

2. Bring out each animal piece for the child to name. Discard any she is unable to name, and replace it with another animal she is able to name. Place the animals outside the farm. Make sure each piece is clearly visible to the child.

3. Explain to the child that all the farmer's animals have escaped: "Can you help the farmer?" "He has lost his animals", and "Let's bring them safely home".

4. Ask the child to find an animal: for example, "Where's the *cow*?"

5. If the child is unsure, repeat the question or use a simpler request, such as "*cow*". It may be necessary to point to the item or use a picture or symbol cue. When the child has correctly selected the animal, she can place it in the farmyard.

6. Continue until all the animals are in the farmyard.

To increase the complexity of the activity

- gradually increase the number of animals the child has to choose between (maximum five to six);
- introduce a delay before the child is allowed to respond.

Variations

- Vary the animals.
- Use a zoo and appropriate animals, rather than a farm.
- Hide the animals around the room.

LISTENING TO SPOKEN LANGUAGE
LISTENING TO SINGLE WORDS: ANIMALS

Activities for Early Years Settings

These games will help children with their listening skills. Although they will help communication skills, they are not designed specifically to teach language. It is expected that the children will know the vocabulary used in the listening activities. These games will help with listening to animal names.

☐ *Noah's Ark*

Make a large cardboard cut-out of Noah's Ark. Draw different animals on the side of the ark. Have matching animal pictures. Ask each child to find the picture of the animal you name and place it with the other animal in the ark. Use Blu-tack or a similar adhesive to secure the pictures.

☐ *Animal race*

Have a race! Give the children different miniature animals that have to jump several hurdles. (Use plastic toy fences from a farm set or make your own with cardboard.) Each animal can only jump a hurdle when its name has been called.

☐ *Picture lotto*

Draw or stick animal pictures on a lotto board. Have matching flashcards. Take one card but do not allow the child to see the picture. Name the animal. The child must point to the animal on the lotto board. If the child is correct, she can have the card to place on the board. (A group of children can play this game and have a competition to see who finishes first.)

☐ *Draw an animal*

Place several plastic animal shapes in the middle of the table. Name an animal for each child to choose and draw round.

☐ *Animal farm*

Ask the children to help you set up a model farm. Use a toy farm and animals. Name the animals you want the children to place on the farm.

☐ *Matching animal shapes to pictures*

You will need several miniature animal pieces with matching animal pictures. Ask the child to find an animal and place it on the matching picture.

LISTENING TO SPOKEN LANGUAGE
LISTENING TO SINGLE WORDS: ANIMALS
Activities for Home

These are games to help your child listen to animal names. For listening activities it is important only to use animals your child knows and can name. Check her understanding of words by asking her to name the animals before you use them in the games.

❑ *Animal noises*

Name an animal. Can she make the appropriate noise, such as "moo" for a cow, "neigh" for a horse?

❑ *Animal masks*

Make large, colourful animal masks. The child puts on the appropriate mask when you name the animal. Encourage her to mime the animal's movements and copy the sounds it makes.

❑ *Visit a farm or zoo*

Ask your child to find different animals as you walk round the farm or zoo. There are many 'city farms' where your child will enjoy stroking and feeding the animals. When you return home, draw a picture of an animal you saw on your visit. Ask your child to draw an animal for you.

❑ *Story books*

Look at animal pictures in a book. Ask your child to find different animals as you name them. You can make the animal sounds together. Useful books include the traditional 'Old MacDonald's Farm' and the Dr. Seuss book 'Mr. Brown Can Moo! Can You?' Apps with an animated, interactive version with sound and music are also available for these books on smartphones and tablets.

❑ *Animal posters*

Find posters or large pictures that portray several different animals in a particular setting: for example a jungle scene or animals at a zoo. Ask your child to point to the animals as you name them.

❑ *Puzzles*

Many early puzzles have animals as a theme. Ask your child to take out and put back the animals you name.

LISTENING TO SPOKEN LANGUAGE
LISTENING TO SINGLE WORDS: ANIMALS

Materials and Equipment

Materials and equipment that can be used to represent animals include the following:

- ❏ soft animal toys
- ❏ animal puppets
- ❏ play dough or clay models
- ❏ papier-mâché models
- ❏ toy plastic animals
- ❏ animal masks
- ❏ cardboard cut-outs
- ❏ pictures from magazines
- ❏ line drawings of single animals
- ❏ picture cards of single animals
- ❏ photo cards of single animals

LISTENING TO SPOKEN LANGUAGE: ACTION WORDS
Teaching Activity

'Make Dolly Dance'

You will need:
a doll with moveable legs and arms.

Useful words and phrases:
look; listen; doll; dance; walk; run; sit down; lie down; jump.

What to do:

1. Introduce the doll to the child. Show her how to move her arms and legs to make her dance, sit, jump, lie down, walk and run.
2. Let the child have a turn at copying these actions with the doll.
3. Ask her to make the doll carry out an action: for example, "Make dolly *dance*".
4. If the child is unsure, repeat the question or use a simpler request, such as "*dance*". It may be necessary to move your body in imitation of dancing or to show the child the action with the doll.
5. Continue with the game until the child has tried several actions.

To increase the complexity of the activity
- ask the child to perform more than one action with the doll: for example, "Make dolly *jump* and *sit down*";
- introduce a delay before the child is allowed to respond.

Variations
- Use a teddy instead of a doll.
- Ask the child to name actions for you to carry out with the doll.

LISTENING TO SPOKEN LANGUAGE: ACTION WORDS
Activities for Early Years Settings

These are games to help children with their listening skills. Although they will help communication skills, they are not designed specifically to teach language. It is expected that the children will know the vocabulary used in the listening activities. These games will help with listening to action words.

☐ *Playground games*

Ask the children to carry out different actions. Try jumping, hopping and skipping.

☐ *Pictures*

Gather together several pictures of people carrying out various actions. Hide these around the room. Ask the children to find different pictures: for example, "Find someone *jumping*?" They can imitate the action when they find the picture.

☐ *Actions*

Use miniature animal figures, which have different positions, such as lying down, sitting, standing or eating. Ask the children to find different animals: "Show me the one *eating*", and so on. (Only have one animal for each action.)

☐ *Obstacle course*

Set up an obstacle course for the children. Let them take turns to go round the course. Ask each child to carry out different actions as they come to an obstacle. For example, a mat can be jumped over, walked round or hopped across.

LISTENING TO SPOKEN LANGUAGE: ACTION WORDS
Activities for Home

These are games to help your child with her listening skills. For listening activities it is important only to use action words your child understands and can name.

☐ *'Simon says'*

Play 'Simon says'. Give your child an action to carry out, such as "*jump*" or "*hop*". Let her have a turn at playing Simon.

☐ *Make dolly jump*

You will need a doll or teddy with movable arms and legs to play this game. Show your child how to make different actions with the doll. Ask your child to make the doll carry out different actions: for example, "make dolly *jump*".

☐ *Ball games*

Ask your child to carry out different actions with a ball. These could include throwing, rolling, kicking and catching.

☐ *Action songs*

Sing action songs with your child. Leave pauses for her to do the actions named in the song. Try 'Hokey Cokey', 'Hop Hop Hop' and 'Monkey See and Monkey Do'. (All are available on Spotify or YouTube.)

LISTENING TO SPOKEN LANGUAGE: ACTION WORDS
Materials and Equipment

Try using the following items in listening games using action words:

- ☐ real people!
- ☐ teddy or other toy with movable limbs
- ☐ plastic animals with movable limbs
- ☐ puppets
- ☐ dolls made from pipe-cleaners
- ☐ pictures from magazines of people carrying out actions
- ☐ photocards of people carrying out actions
- ☐ line drawings of people carrying out actions

LISTENING TO SPOKEN LANGUAGE
Listening to Simple Commands

The complexity of a command or instruction will be determined by one or more of the following: (1) number of information carrying words, (2) length of sentence and (3) concepts.

Sentences that involve two information carrying words have at least two key words within the sentence that the child must understand before she can carry out the command or instruction appropriately. Activities will involve the child in making a choice for each of these key words. For example, the command, "Give me the *red book*" may involve the use of a red book, a blue book, a red pencil and a blue pencil. The child must choose between the book and the pencil and the colours red and blue. (Note that if you hold out your hand, she does not have to understand the word 'give'.)

Some simple commands can make use of the child's everyday knowledge of events. The command, "Put the *doll* on the *chair*" only has two information carrying words (if the child has to choose between another toy and another item of furniture). The word 'on' is redundant as it is usual for people to sit on a chair. Therefore, the child does not need to understand this word to carry out the command correctly. Once a different preposition is introduced, as in "Put the *doll under* the *chair*" or "Put the *teddy behind* the *table*", the child has to understand three words and the command becomes more complex.

The length of the sentence can be increased by asking the child to fetch two items, as in "Bring me *dolly* and *teddy*". Other sentences could include "Show me"; "Give me"; "Put the"; "Find the" and "Where are". Names can also be used to increase length, as with "Find Farouk and Jessie, please". (See section 8 on Auditory Memory for more ideas on similar activities.)

A simple command may include one or more of the following concepts (remember this will also increase the memory load):

- size (big, large, small, little)
- length (long, short)
- weight (heavy, light)
- position (under, on, in, next to, behind, near to)
- action words (jump, run, hop, skip, clap)
- colour (red, yellow, blue, orange)
- shape (round, square)
- number (one, two, three, many, few, lots)
- texture (smooth, shiny, rough)

Section 9: Listening to Spoken Language

The activities used in 'Listening to Single Words' can be modified to include more complex instructions.

Examples of activities

◆ Obstacle race

Ask the child to carry out different actions with different obstacles. For example, "*Crawl* under the *table*"; "*Run to* the *hoop*"; "*Walk* to the *chair*".

◆ Tidy up time

Use commands that involve prepositions, such as "Put your bag *under* the *bed*" or "Put your football *behind* the *chair*". Make sure you hand the child the object (bag, football, etc.) before you give the instruction.

◆ Animals in their place

Use miniature animals and a farm layout with buildings and fields. Ask the child to place one of the animals in a part of the farm: for example, "Put the *cow* in the *field*".

Ask the child to place the animal in an unexpected place, for example, "Put the *cow* in the *pond*".

◆ Moving Day

Play a pretend game of moving house. Ask the child to place pieces of furniture in a room in the new house: for example, "Put the *chair* in the *living room*". Ask the child to place the furniture in an unexpected place: for example, "Put the *bath* in the *bedroom* ". Pretend to be removal people. (You could wrap the furniture in paper or put the items in boxes!)

LISTENING TO SPOKEN LANGUAGE
Listening to Complex Commands

A complex command or instruction will have one or more of the following constituents: (1) multiple information carrying words, (2) increased length of sentence, (3) complexity and (4) a number of concepts.

The child is required to understand at least three information carrying words within the sentence before she can carry out the command or instruction appropriately. The activity will need to be structured so that the child has to make a choice for each of the key words. For example, the command, "Put the *doll under* the *bed*" may involve the use of a doll, a teddy, a bed and a table. The child must choose between the doll and the teddy, and between the table and the bed. The preposition 'under' is also an information carrying word as the doll could also go in, on top of, behind or next to the bed. Remember to contrast prepositions and use unusual positions; otherwise the child can use her everyday knowledge of events to guess that the doll goes 'in' the bed.

The length of the sentence can also be increased by asking the child to fetch several items, as with, "Bring me an apple, an orange, a pear and a banana, please". Other sentences could include, "Show me"; "Give me"; "Put the"; "Find the" and "Where are". The children's names can also be used to increase the length, as in "Touch Chen, Peter, Mita and Karolina, please". (See section 8 on Auditory Memory for more ideas on similar activities.)

The type of grammatical constructions used in the sentence will affect complexity. A sentence with a subject, verb, object (SVO) construction is a simple format that can easily be developed into a complex command. "The cow is in the field" can be used as the basis of "Put the black cow in the field". Compare the complex grammatical instruction, "Put the book, lying on the red table, in the tray" with the simpler type of command, "Put the book in the tray". Start with simpler grammatical constructions, and gradually introduce more complex commands.

A complex command may include one or more of the following concepts (remember this will also increase the memory load):

- size (big, large, small, little)
- length (long, short)
- weight (heavy, light)
- position (under, on, in, next to, behind, near to)
- action words (jump, run, hop, skip, clap)
- colour (red, yellow, blue, orange)
- shape (round, square)

Section 9: Listening to Spoken Language

- number (one, two, three, many, few, lots)
- texture (smooth, shiny, rough)

The activities used in 'Listening to Single Words' can be modified to include more complex instructions.

Examples of activities

- Shopping game

Ask the child to "Buy a *big apple* and put it in a *bag*".
  There should be a big and a small apple amongst the food items. Similarly there should be a choice between a bag and another type of container, like a basket or a box. As well as size, you can use 'number' and 'weight'. For example: "*two bananas*" or the "*heaviest potato*".

- Teddy's going on holiday

Ask the child to "Put teddy's *red jumper* in his *duffle bag*".
  There should be a red and a blue jumper amongst the clothes items. Similarly there should be a choice between a duffle bag and another type of luggage, like a suitcase or backpack. As well as colour, you can use 'texture' or 'length'. For example: "*short scarf*" or his "*shiny shorts*".

- Give dolly a bath

Ask the child to "*Wash dolly's hands*".
  Include another toy like a teddy with the dolly. Use different action words like 'dry' 'brush' and 'clean'.

- Obstacle race

Ask the child to carry out actions and then move to a named place. For example, "Touch your *nose* and *walk* to the *window*".
  The complexity can be increased as you include more choices: "*Rub* your *nose* and *walk* to the *window*"; "*Rub* your *head* and *run* to the *door*". In this activity the child has a choice of *body part*; *action* on that body part; *place*; and *action to get to the place*.

LISTENING TO SPOKEN LANGUAGE
Record Sheet

Child's name	

Date	Activity/context	Observations
Example 4.5.	*(Child's name) is sitting with a small group of children playing 'Shops'. Joined by a teaching assistant who asks for some food items for a picnic. (AI)*	*(Child's name) selected some single items of food like 'cake' and 'drink'. Simple commands using two food items needed to be broken down into single elements.*

AI = adult initiated activity; CI = child initiated activity

SECTION 10
Listening Skills in the Curriculum

Topics 197

LISTENING SKILLS IN THE CURRICULUM
Topics

The following ideas can be used to help develop the children's listening skills in relation to topics within the Early Years Foundation Stage (EYFS) and Key Stage 1 (KS1).

Musical instruments

Links with EYFS Communication and Language (Listening and Attention); KS1 Music, and KS1 Science.

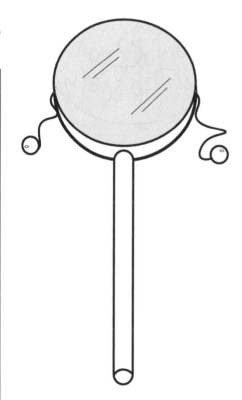

Children can:

- explore a wide range of pitched (/tuned) and unpitched (/untuned) percussion instruments;
- discover the different ways of making sound with musical instruments (shaking, tapping, hitting, plucking, blowing);
- experiment with unusual ways of playing an instrument: for example, stroking a drum instead of hitting it or rubbing a maraca on the floor.;
- make their own instrument, like a rainmaker, shekere, didgeridoo or Chinese gong. Links to other curriculum topics can be made: for example, rainmaker with 'weather' or Chinese gong with Chinese New Year;
- explore a different instrument group each week;
- tap out the syllables in a simple song using a musical instrument like a maraca or rhythm sticks;
- create an eBook using the Book Creator app for tablets that includes photos and sound recordings of their music making with different instruments;
- use musical instruments to 'paint a sound picture' of a busy high street or a nature trail;
- learn to make sound effects to accompany a story;
- investigate sound and vibrations, for example, rice bouncing around on a drum head;
- listen to Evelyn Glenie (deaf percussionist) talk about how she hears through her whole body at: https://www.youtube.com/watch?v=IU3V6zNER4g

Section 10: Listening Skills in the Curriculum

Music

Links with EYFS Understanding the World (People and Communities) and Communication and Language (Listening and Attention), KS1 Music and KS1 Drama.

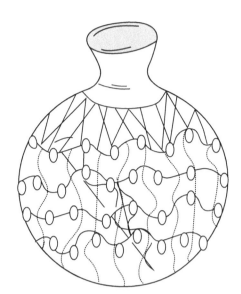

Children can:

☐ listen to live music from invited musicians performing music from different genres and cultures;

☐ compare two interpretations of a pop song (the children may be surprised to hear an older version of a 'new' pop song);

☐ bring in recordings of music that are important or well known in their culture;

☐ see and hear how music is used in drama by visiting a theatre or having an invited group of performers visit;

☐ learn turn-taking and waiting for a cue (voice and visual) in circle group activities for music;

☐ take turns at conducting a music session with simple tasks like getting others to start and stop, or increase and decrease volume, go quick or slow;

☐ make up their own music, using poems or stories to stimulate ideas;

☐ discuss the similarities and differences between two different pieces of music using musical elements like pitch, rhythm and timbre.

☐ listen to instrumental music that reflects a range of moods like Peter and the Wolf;

☐ create a simple dance or set of movements with a partner to fit a piece of music, each pair performing in front of the other children

Singing

Links with EYFS Understanding the World (People and Communities) and Communication and Language (Listening and Attention), KS1 History and KS1 Music.

Children can:

☐ feel the vibration as they sing low to high notes by putting the back of the hand gently against the throat just under the chin;

Section 10: Listening Skills in the Curriculum

- learn a well-known folk song and perform it for other children;
- ask parents to record traditional songs;
- regularly record their singing and listen back to make some simple 'critical' judgements of their work;
- make up their own songs by building on a familiar tune or song, for example, adding new words to a familiar tune or extending a favourite song with new verses. (Vocabulary can be linked to a curriculum topic).
- ask their grandparents what music and songs they liked when they were the same age;
- learn a song related to an historical event; for example, World War One;
- learn to sing and sign

Environment

Links with EYFS Understanding the World (People and Communities) and Communication and Language (Listening and Attention); KS1 Music.

Children can:

- talk about the sounds they hear at school and compare these with the sounds they hear at home or in their local street;
- use a tablet to record different sounds they hear on a nature walk;
- look at the way sounds in the environment change with the seasons ('Listen, Listen' by Phillis Gershator, a book about sounds in different seasons, is a good book to support this);
- recreate the sounds of a thunder storm through musical instruments and recorded water play sounds;
- create a musical notation by drawing symbols to represent individual sounds: for example, a big splash of water colour paint for rain. Symbols can be re-arranged to create different sequences of sound;
- compare the natural sounds of the environment with those made by man;
- talk about why they love some sounds but not others;
- build a 'sound' sensory walk outside: for example, wind chimes, plants with seed pods that rattle in the wind, rustling sounds from grasses and bamboo; various objects to hit with sticks.

Section 10: Listening Skills in the Curriculum

Communication

Links with EYFS Understanding the World (People and Communities) and Communication and Language (Listening and Attention), PSHE, KS1 Science and KS1 Music.

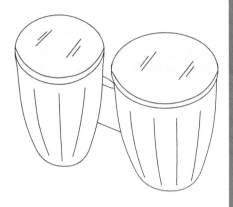

Children can:

- ☐ make a recording of all the different sounds the class can make using their voices, tongues, cheeks, teeth and lips;

- ☐ experiment with communicating one message using different means, including verbal and non-verbal methods, for example 'go' could be shouted, signalled by a raised flag, a hooter, a green card or the written word;

- ☐ beat out a message on a drum: for example, by tapping a drum on every syllable, so "Hello" would be two quick beats, "How are you?" would be three beats evenly spaced;

- ☐ learn sign language and have a finger spelling competition, where the children have to learn to spell a certain number of words;

- ☐ learn how to say a greeting in different languages – children who speak other languages can share their knowledge;

- ☐ can read about listening and speaking with books like 'The Ear Book' by Al Perkins, 'I Listen' by Cheri J. Meiners, 'Telephone' by Mac Barnett and 'Yes, I Can Listen!' by Steve Metzger;

- ☐ discover books that reflect diversity through positive representations: for example, 'Jake and Jasmine to the Rescue' by Karen Harlow has the hero character Jake who wears a cochlear implant (a NDCS publication).

SECTION 11
Holiday Projects

Introduction 203

Holiday Listening Projects 204

INTRODUCTION

This *section* has numerous suggestions for reinforcing the child's listening skills and expanding her auditory experiences. Activities range from special visits to places of interest to more everyday experiences such as attending a playgroup or a walk in the park. These activities are aimed at parents, carers or others in close contact with the child who may want to continue working on the child's listening skills during holidays. Some ideas may be new, while others may reassure users that the activities in which the child already participates will enhance her listening skills. There should be an activity to suit everyone, regardless of financial or social needs. Some are for whole family participation and others are for the individual child.

HOLIDAY PROJECTS
Holiday Listening Projects

Below are some ideas for helping your child's listening skills during the holidays. They include places to visit, special events and ideas of how you can join in the fun. Check your local paper for dates of special activities or details of places to visit. There is often a lot of information at your local library about up and coming events. Look out for free entry or special rates for children.

☐ *Walk in the park*

Listen to all the sounds you can hear on a walk in the park. You can make your own sounds by splashing in puddles, dragging a stick along the railings or copying the sounds of any birds or animals you see.

Record the sounds from your walk on your phone or tablet for listening and talking about later. Remember to take some photos to go with your sound recording.

☐ *Farm or zoo*

Visit your local zoo or farm to listen to the different animal and bird sounds. Help your child to record these sounds on your phone or tablet.

Make a digital book using a Book Creator app on your tablet to help remember your visit. Photographs and sound recordings can be uploaded to the eBook, and your child can add recordings of her own voice copying the animal sounds.

☐ *Storytime at the library*

Many libraries have a special time during the day when stories are read aloud for children. This helps the child with listening and concentration, as well as introducing her to storybooks. Look out for Sensory Storytimes, which provide a safe and inclusive experience for children who may have autism or sensory processing difficulties. They provide appropriate support for these children and offer a more interactive approach involving books, songs, music as well as fun games like blowing bubbles.

☐ *Special days*

Many local councils, community centres, hospitals, schools and day nurseries organize or take part in special event days for users of their services. Activities range from fun days to sports competitions. Whatever the theme, it is guaranteed to stimulate the senses, including the eyes and ears.

Section 11: Holiday Projects

❑ *Puppet shows*

Children love puppet shows with their fun stories and colourful characters. Children will enjoy listening to the different voices while watching the action!

❑ *Clowns*

Clowning is a comic form of mime, which children all over the world love to watch. Although clowns have no speech, there are lots of bangs, whooshes and honks to interest your child. There are also more and more opportunities for children to participate in 'clown' workshops. Check your local library for information.

❑ *Music workshops*

Check out your local orchestra for family friendly days that introduce children to music making through interactive fun workshops.

❑ *Dance exhibitions*

These can be organized events that your child may wish to take part in or a spontaneous expression by street entertainers. Remember that music must accompany the dancing, so your child is listening as well as watching.

❑ *Parades or carnivals*

Watch the colourful procession and listen to the music! You may want to join in with the dancing or singing. Your child can march along with a big brass band. Or she can skip, dance and clap to the strong beat of Afro-Caribbean music.

❑ *Funfairs*

Children of all ages love funfairs. There are many sights, sounds and smells to excite your child before she even takes her first ride. Many sounds are associated with the ride itself – the music of the carousel and the thump as the bumper cars crash. Look out for mini funfairs set up at festive times of the year, or find some at the seaside where they are often found on the end of the pier.

❑ *Something new*

If you are on holiday or visiting your family in another country, your child will experience many new and different sounds. You do not have to go abroad to give your child new experiences. A different town, a new house or even a different routine can stimulate your child's interest in the sounds around her.

❑ *Special exhibitions at museums*

Most museums now have areas designed specifically for children. Displays are placed at an appropriate height, and interaction is encouraged. They

Section 11: Holiday Projects

stimulate all the senses, including sight, sound and touch. Look out for special exhibitions during the holidays.

☐ *Living history museums*

The 'living history museum' is a popular way to discover about life in the past and to find out about the history of a specific area. There are opportunities for children to take part in immersive and interactive activities, where the child can hear, feel, smell and see the past. So a horseshoe is hammered out in a Victorian smithy, and music plays on an old gramophone. Some places to visit are:

Beamish (www.beamish.org.uk), Beamish, County Durham, England. Tells the story of life in North East England during the 1820s, 1900s and 1940s.

The Black Country Living Museum (www.bclm.co.uk), Dudley, Birmingham, England. Tells the story of the role of the Black Country in the Industrial Revolution.

Blists Hill Victorian Town (www.ironbridge.org.uk/explore/blists-hill-victorian-town/), Ironbridge, Shropshire, England. Recreates the everyday life and work of a Victorian town.

New Lanark World Heritage Site (www.newlanark.org), New Lanark, South Lanarkshire, Scotland. An 18th century mill village situated on the River Clyde.

St. Fagans Museum (museum.wales/stfagans/) Cardiff, Wales. Explores the heritage and culture of Wales, showcasing traditional crafts and activities.

Weald and Downland Museum (www.wealddown.co.uk), Singleton, West Sussex, England. Tells the story of rural life in South East England over 1,000 years.

☐ *Historical sound and light shows*

These types of show are becoming increasingly popular. They consist of reconstructions of scenes from the past, using lifelike models with special effects from sound and light. This way your child can see, hear, feel and smell the past. Some famous ones in the United Kingdom include Canterbury Tales at Canterbury (www.canterburytales.org.uk) and Orvik Viking Centre in York (www.jorvikvikingcentre.co.uk). As these can be expensive, you might like to save this activity for a treat.

☐ *Children's theatre and drama groups*

Do you have any local theatre workshops or drama groups for children? Taking part in a children's theatre will involve your child in exploring and experimenting with her voice. It will also be beneficial for the development of her social, language and communication skills.

Section 11: Holiday Projects

☐ *Playgroups*

Here your child will meet other children and have the opportunity to take part in a variety of activities that are not feasible at home, such as hand and foot painting! These organizations may also provide outings for your child that will expand her listening experience.

☐ *Art galleries*

Many artists are engaged with developing multisensory experiences that combine movement with sound and visual special effects. Check out events designed specifically for young children.

SECTION 12
Listening Resources

Introduction..211

Teaching Guidelines... 212

Listening Resources: Early Years Settings......................... 213

INTRODUCTION

A *varied* auditory experience is vital in building children's understanding of objects and events in the world around them. This knowledge provides a foundation for the development of *language, communication and the ability to create and think critically*.

This section has ideas about how to create an *enabling environment* for the development of auditory skills. The focus is on providing opportunities for child-initiated activities that encourage *exploration* and *active play* with a variety of sound makers, musical instruments and audio-visual material.

Some children may need support and guidance from the adult in attending to and making sense of what they hear. Adults can stimulate interest through shared attention and build on child-initiated play as a basis for planned activities.

LISTENING RESOURCES
Teaching Guidelines

Support children with a hearing loss by:

- recognizing each child is unique and may respond to an auditory experience by listening, watching or feeling (vibration), or a combination of all these ways;
- providing a variety of stimulating sound makers, musical instruments and auditory-visual material;
- understanding that a single singer or one instrument might be easier to follow than several instruments or singing with music;
- making music accessible for all: for example, providing immobile children with sound makers and musical instruments you can play lying down;
- ensuring that resources are relevant to all the children's cultures and communities (including the Deaf community);
- repeating experiences to help consolidate the child's learning;
- using assistive technology where appropriate to enhance the child's experience of music.*

*Seek the advice of a teacher of the deaf, educational audiologist or specialist speech and language therapist about assistive technologies such as wireless (for example, neck loops, Bluetooth streamers) and direct audio input devices.

Read more information on technology on the National Deaf Children's Society website: www.ndcs.org.uk/family_support/technology

LISTENING RESOURCES
Early Years Settings

Provide a variety of stimulating auditory experiences that support and encourage the child to *explore* and engage through *active play,* and provide opportunities to be *creative and think critically.*

☐ *Listening box*

Make your own listening resource box. Collect together interesting sound makers, and keep them together in a large box for children to *explore* and use in *active listening*. Ask the children's families for ideas about musical instruments and sound makers so that your collection represents different cultures and musical genres.

Here are some suggestions to get you started:

- ☐ maracas with LED lights
- ☐ reflective tambourine
- ☐ large ocean drum
- ☐ squeaky toys
- ☐ shakers
- ☐ rattle
- ☐ clatter-pillar
- ☐ rainmaker
- ☐ groan tube
- ☐ rhythm sticks
- ☐ boomwhackers
- ☐ carousel spinning top
- ☐ material that makes a noise, for example, paper to crunch
- ☐ sand blocks
- ☐ musical mobiles
- ☐ music box
- ☐ wind up tin music box
- ☐ alarm clock (vibrating and light up ones)
- ☐ metronome
- ☐ buzzers
- ☐ hooters
- ☐ bells
- ☐ wind chimes
- ☐ musical cards
- ☐ musical toys
- ☐ books with sound makers, such as buzzers
- ☐ echo microphone
- ☐ cardboard tubes

Section 12: Listening Resources

☐ *Create a music corner*

Create a dedicated space for music, similar to a book corner, but the focus is on sound making, music and vocalization. Use the space for planned adult led activities, but also as a space where children can independently explore different sound makers and musical instruments. Here are some suggested activities:

- Have a weekly musical treasure basket – use selected items from your listening resource box to fill a treasure basket for children to explore sound making independently. Some ideas are:

    - shakers using a variety of everyday items (rice, Lego bricks, shells) in see-through/opaque plastic containers (with lids firmly secured shut)
    - items to tap together (two shells, two wooden sticks)
    - different types of one musical instrument: for example, 'bells' might include sleigh bells, hand bells, Tibetan bells
    - instruments that require different hand movements: for example, a maraca to shake, a triangle to strike, rhythm sticks to tap, a drum to beat, a guiro to scrape, sand blocks to rub together and an afuche cabasa to twist.
    - instruments where you need two hands like Tibetan bells, a guiro or a tulip block with beater
    - instruments with contrasting sounds: for example, the continuous sound of a shaker with the intermittent sound of a drum beat

- Vocal play – encourage singing and vocal play by providing resources children can vocalise into: for example, echo microphones, cardboard tubing and kazoos.
- A huddle table – encourage interaction and social music making by providing a table or large box with space around it so children can gather round or 'huddle'. Set out pairs of instruments and sound makers for children to explore together.

☐ *Hang a musical washing line*

Use homemade musical instruments and everyday sound makers to hang on a washing line in your outside space. See 'How to make a musical washing line' at https://www.tes.com/news/how-make-musical-washing-line.

☐ *Audio stories and songs*

Provide a place for children to listen to recorded versions of familiar rhymes, songs and stories. Use audio books, eBooks, apps, and sites like Storynory.com to find suitable material.

Children can listen alone, with another child, in a group or do the activities with an adult who can prompt her if necessary. Collect different toys and materials for the child to play with while listening to the recordings.

Section 12: Listening Resources

Here are some suggestions:

Rhymes

- 'Two Little Dickie Birds sitting on a Wall' – have two finger puppets for the child to wear as she sings along with the rhyme.
- 'Humpty Dumpty Sat on a Wall' – a soft toy in the shape of Humpty Dumpty can be bought from toyshops. He can fall off a table, the back of a chair or a box.
- 'Twinkle, Twinkle Little Star' – have a selection of star or fairy wands that light up or wrist bells that tinkle as the child gestures 'star'.

Songs

- 'Old MacDonald's Farm' – give the child a set of miniature animals to hold or some animal hand puppets to wear.
- 'The Wheels on the Bus' – use a large floor puzzle of a bus for the child to piece together. Play the song and see if she can point to the wheels, the passengers on the bus and so on.
- 'Ring-a-Ring-of-Roses' – the child can dance to the music or act out the song with a puppet.

Stories

- 'The Gingerbread Man' – cut out lots of felt or paper buttons, hats and ribbons for the child to decorate some brown cardboard gingerbread dolls.
- 'Little Red Riding Hood' – have some dressing up clothes and props, like a cloak and picnic basket.
- 'Three Billy Goats Gruff' – encourage role-play with stick puppets.
- 'Three Little Pigs' – lay out some LEGO bricks for house building.
- 'Jungle Book' – have animal facemasks for the child to wear.
- 'Green Eggs and Ham' by Dr. Seuss – draw some simple egg shapes, the child can add the green yolk with a paint marker.

Find out what rhymes, songs and stories children hear at home, and include these in your resource area.

Music through stories

Introduce different genres and styles of music to the children through familiar books.

For example, link:

- 'We're Going on a Bear Hunt' by Helen Oxenbury and Michael Rosen to 'Teddy Bear's Picnic' by Henry Hall
- 'Little Green Frog: Chunky Lift a Flap Board Book' by Ginger Swift to 'Five Green and Speckled Frogs' (nursery rhyme)
- 'Buzzy the Bumblebee' by Denise Brennan-Nelson to the 'Flight of the Bumblebee' by Nikolai Rimsky-Korsakov

Copyright material from Diana Williams (2020), *Early Listening Skills for Children with a Hearing Loss*, Second Edition, Routledge

Section 12: Listening Resources

Sign and sing

Explore using sign with singing. The use of signing in early years settings will benefit children's language development, communication skills, build confidence and self-expression. Using sign as you sing will encourage all children to participate, and it will also support those children who use signing as their preferred method of communication. Staff can train in the use of sign with singing (for example, Makaton www.makaton.org/training/singing), or a sign and sing professional might be invited into your setting on a regular basis.

Movement with music

Moving to music will help make children more aware of the sounds they are hearing and help them to listen too. Create space to allow for movement with musical instruments and sound makers.

- Encourage the children to make different movements with different musical sounds, for example, march to a drumbeat, walk on tiptoe to sleigh bells or jump to a frog guiro.
- Encourage the children to move whilst playing their instruments, for example, marching while tapping rhythm sticks together.
- Help children explore different ways to make sounds by moving their instruments; for example, shaking a maraca high up in the air, then down on the ground, next to each side of their body and finally making a circle in the air.
- Play an instrument or piece of music, and invite the children to move in response.

Here are some ideas of musical instruments, sound makers and other resources that will encourage movement or dance to music.

- Hoops
- Ribbon rings
- Pompoms
- Parachute
- Tinsel
- Wrist and ankle bells
- Rainmakers
- Boomwhackers
- Large ocean drum
- Egg shakers
- Maracas
- Tambourine
- Afuche Cabasa

☐ *Mark making with music*

Encourage mark making to music using different mediums. Here are a few ideas for materials for mark making:

- sand on a light box;
- finger paints;
- gloop;
- trains and cars to roll through thick paint;
- string and paint for printing, dragging and dripping;
- scrapers and miniature rakes in a damp sand box;
- prints made with corks or other similar objects;
- washing up sponges or squeegees with watered down paints;
- roller and paint trays with large sheets of paper;
- pushing different objects into play dough or clay;
- cotton reels – paint the edges or sides for printing or rolling;
- dripping paint from large brushes;
- sticks and twigs to put mud on fabric sheets;
- water sprayers on large sheets of paper.

Introduce different types of music to accompany the mark making. Which ones are suited to large sweeping gestures? Which were the best to accompany quiet activities like the sand and light box? Does any music make you think of drips or rain? How do the children respond to fast music?

SECTION 13
Sounds, Sound Makers and Musical Instruments

Introduction *221*

Musical Instruments *222*

Homemade Instruments *233*

Shakers *234*

Home Sounds *235*

Human Sounds *236*

Animal Sounds *237*

Environmental Sounds *238*

Action Sounds *241*

INTRODUCTION

This section provides a comprehensive list of sounds, sound makers and musical instruments for use in listening activities. Using a variety of sounds and sound makers will help the child to generalize her listening skills. The check boxes can be used to indicate appropriate sounds and sound makers for a specific child.

SOUNDS, SOUND MAKERS AND MUSICAL INSTRUMENTS
Musical Instruments

Percussion instruments are an ideal choice for listening activities. Some instruments are heavy and difficult to manipulate, so consider buying a mini or early years version. Always check manufacturer's recommended age range for use.

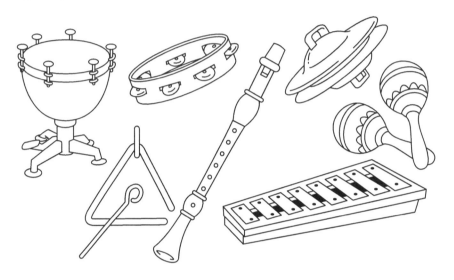

Bells

Name	Description	Characteristic	Origin
☐ carousel rainbow bells	Eight colourful bells mounted on a carousel stand. Each bell plays a different note when struck with a mallet.	Single notes or a continuous sound of different notes when spun. Possible to play simple nursery rhymes.	Educational toy
☐ double agogo bell	Two metal cone shaped bells with two tones. One relatively higher than the other.	Hold with the bells facing away. Strike with a wooden or metal beater to make a cowbell sound. Use for rhythmic patterns.	West Africa (Yoruba)/ Brazil
☐ handbells	Hand held bells with different notes.	Continuous sound or can be played to follow a beat.	England/ America

222   Copyright material from Diana Williams (2020), *Early Listening Skills for Children with a Hearing Loss*, Second Edition, Routledge

Section 13: Sounds, Sound Makers and Musical Instruments

Name	Description	Characteristic	Origin
☐ sleigh bells !	20+ jingle bells attached to a wooden block with handle.	Hold downwards with a clenched fist. (This hold keeps bells silent.) Hit the hand holding the handle with the fist of the other hand.	Europe
☐ mini sleigh bells !	Three to five jingle bells attached to a handgrip.	Continuous sound or can be played to follow the beat. Difficult to keep quiet.	Modern
☐ Tibetan bells	Small metal cymbals. Strike the edges together.	Long, continuous, high pitched sound.	Tibet
☐ wrist and ankle bells !	Bells on a strap worn on wrist or ankle.	Continuous sound associated with movement. Clapping or stomping creates a rhythm.	India

 Small jingle bells are a choking hazard. Check instruments regularly to make sure bells are not coming loose.

Castanets

Name	Description	Characteristic	Origin
☐ castanets	A pair of wooden or plastic concave shallow bowls held together with a cord.	Fast rhythmic patterns.	Europe/ Spain
☐ stick castanet (clapper)	Castanet on a stick.	Shake or strike against the palm or the thigh. Makes a continuous rattling sound or a clap when struck.	Modern

Chime bars

Name	Description	Characteristic	Origin
☐ glockenspiel	Tuned metal bars arranged like a keyboard. Smaller and higher in pitch than the xylophone.	Some are colour coded. Useful for learning about pitch or rhythmic patterns.	Europe (Germany) Also see xylophone

Section 13: Sounds, Sound Makers and Musical Instruments

Name	Description	Characteristic	Origin
☐ metal chime bars	Metal bar mounted on a wooden resonator box.	Played with a mallet. Can hold in hand. Each bar has a different tone. Good for learning about pitch or beat.	Europe
☐ resonator bars	Wooden bar mounted on an acoustically accurate tone chamber. Come in bass, contra bass and sub contra.	Excellent sound for those with hearing loss. Good substitute for timpani drum.	Modern
☐ triangles	Metal, triangular shape, suspended on a string. Large size has a low tone. Small size has a high tone. Strike with a metal bar.	Long vibration. Use for rhythmic beats. Need to have some coordination to play, as need to suspend.	Europe
☐ wooden chime bars	Wooden bar mounted on a wooden resonator.	Played with a mallet. Each bar has a different tone. Good for learning about pitch or rhythmic patterns.	Europe
☐ xylophone	Wooden bars arranged over tuned wooden resonators. Notes arranged like a keyboard.	Some are colour coded. Useful for learning about pitch or rhythmic patterns. Worth paying for a percussion instrument rather than a toy xylophone.	Europe adapted from traditional African/Asian instruments

Cymbals

Name	Description	Characteristic	Origin
☐ cymbals	Two flat circular metal discs. Strike together, or gently rub each disc against the other. Or suspend by the handle and hit with a mallet.	Use a mallet to make a loud sound, or tap repeatedly gradually building a crescendo of sound. Good for music and movement.	Asia

Section 13: Sounds, Sound Makers and Musical Instruments

	finger cymbals	Pair of small cymbals held with the thumb and middle finger. Different sizes and materials create different sounds.	Used in belly dancing and played like castanets. Small cymbals can be used in a similar way to full size cymbals.	Turkey/ Middle East

Drums

Name		Description	Characteristic	Origin
☐	bongo drums	Two different sized drums. The larger drum is called the hembra, and the smaller one is called the macho.	Mainly played with the hands. Produces a relatively high pitch compared with other Latin American drum – e.g. conga drum.	Afro-Cuban
☐	djembe	Shaped like a goblet. Tuned by ropes.	Wide range of pitches when head of drum is struck in different places.	West Africa
☐	hand drums	Hand held but can be played between the knees.	Play with the hands or a soft mallet.	Africa
☐	ocean drum	Two headed drum with small balls inside that roll around to give an ocean wave sound. One side is transparent, and the other is fabric.	Good multisensory instrument. Lightweight, good for encouraging movement. Hold horizontally or vertically and gently tilt.	Native American (water drum)
☐	tabla	Pair of small drums. Small right hand (treble), usually wood. Larger left hand (base), usually metal. Played with the fingers and palm.	Fast rhythmic patterns. Complicated to play.	India
☐	tambour	Hand held drum with a covering or skin on one side of a round frame. Like a large tambourine without the jingles.	Good for exploring different ways of playing. Tap with fingers or a beater, or rub fingers gently across the skin.	Europe/ Middle East

Section 13: Sounds, Sound Makers and Musical Instruments

Name	Description	Characteristic	Origin
☐ timpani (kettle drum)	Large bowl shaped drum in various sizes. Come in sets of 2–5. A tuned or pitched sound.	Each drum in a set has a different pitch. Very expensive, but a good pitched sound if available in your setting.	Europe/ Middle East

Scrapers

Name	Description	Characteristic	Origin
☐ frog guiro	Hand made from solid wood, in the shape of a frog with ridges on its back. Come in several different sizes.	Striker is brushed across the ridges from back to front to produce a croaking sound. Use it as a tone block by tapping on its head.	Thailand
☐ fish guiro	Long, fish shaped, hollow, wooden body with a ribbed surface. Hold in palm of hand. Some have holes for thumb and finger placement.	Play by tapping the beater on the body, or by rubbing the beater across the ribbed notches to make a rasping sound. Scrape slowly, quickly or in a rhythmic pattern.	Latin America/ Cuba

Shakers

Name	Description	Characteristic	Origin
☐ afuche cabasa (or cabasa)	Loops of metal beads wrapped around a ribbed metal cylinder attached to a handle.	Shake, hit against palm or hold beads with one hand and twist to make a scrapping sound.	Latin America
☐ egg shakers	Egg shaped shaker filled with beads or seeds. Good for small hands.	Shake up and down, back and forth or side to side to create different sounds. Turn it in a round motion for a rolling sound. Vary pitch by changing from a closed grip to an open one.	Latin America
☐ jingle stick	Jingles mounted in a frame with a handle.	Shaken or tapped in the hand to create the classic jingle sound.	Modern

Section 13: Sounds, Sound Makers and Musical Instruments

Name	Description	Characteristic	Origin
☐ maracas	Round or oval hand held shakers with stick handles. Play one or one in each hand. LED flashing maracas available from specialist providers.	Shake back and forth. Hold handles and play as if drumming. Turn it in a round motion for a rolling sound. Long continuous sounds or short beats. Good for music and movement.	Latin America/ Afro-Cuban
☐ rain-maker	Tubular rattle. (Originally constructed from a cactus and its spines!)	Sounds like falling rain when turned over. Transparent tubes add a visual element.	South America
☐ shekere	Hollow gourd covered with a net of shells or beads.	Shaker or rattle sounds. Hit bottom to get a bass sound.	West Africa (Yoruba)

Tambourines

Name	Description	Characteristic	Origin
☐ headless tambourine (jingle ring)	Tambourine without a membrane (drum head) stretched across the frame.	Tap on the palm of the hand for rhythmic patterns, or shake for a continuous rattle.	Europe-
☐ tambourine	Cylindrical frame covered with a membrane or drumhead. Frame has pairs of loose metal jingles.	It can be shaken, struck on either side of the membrane with a mallet or tapped with the fingers and hand in a number of ways.	Middle East

Tone blocks

Name	Description	Characteristic	Origin
☐ rhythm sticks or claves	Two wooden sticks that make a short, clear and precise sound when tapped together.	Good for tapping a beat or rhythmic pattern.	Afro-Cuban
☐ slit drums	Box shape with one or more slits in the top.	Pitch varies with number and size of slits.	Africa

Section 13: Sounds, Sound Makers and Musical Instruments

	Name	Description	Characteristic	Origin
☐	tulip block	Tulip shaped wooden block on a stick. (Large slit in block.) Makes a clear, hollow wooden sound when struck with a mallet.	Tap a beat or rhythmic pattern with a wooden beater.	America/ Latin America
☐	two tone blocks	Two (sometimes three or more) pitched wooden 'bells' or blocks with corrugated sides. Agogo sound.	Hit with a wooden beater, or scratch the sides to make a similar sound to the guiro. Good for tapping a beat or rhythmic pattern. Can alternate from one to the other for a galloping sound.	Africa (Yoruba)/ Brazil
☐	wood block	Hollowed out rectangular piece of wood with a slit in the side. Some have handles. (Smaller version of the slit drum.)	Tap a beat or rhythmic pattern with a wooden beater.	America/ Latin America

Wind instruments

Name	Description	Characteristic	Origin
☐ mouth organ (harmonica)	Small rectangular shape with air chambers and a row of reeds that vibrate to make sound.	Lips are placed over the air chambers. Blow or suck air to create sounds.	In various forms worldwide
☐ recorder	Known as a duct flute. Mouthpiece is restricted with a fipple or plug.	Opening or closing finger holes varies pitch.	Europe
☐ water flute	Water flutes for bath time.	Fill with different amounts of water to produce different notes.	Educational toy
☐ swanee whistle (slide whistle)	Has a fipple like a recorder and a tube with a piston inside. Pitch is changed as you blow into it, by the piston, or slide, moving in and out.	Associated with the children's programme 'The Clangers'. Useful for experimenting with pitch.	Based on piston flutes found in Asia, Africa and Europe

Section 13: Sounds, Sound Makers and Musical Instruments

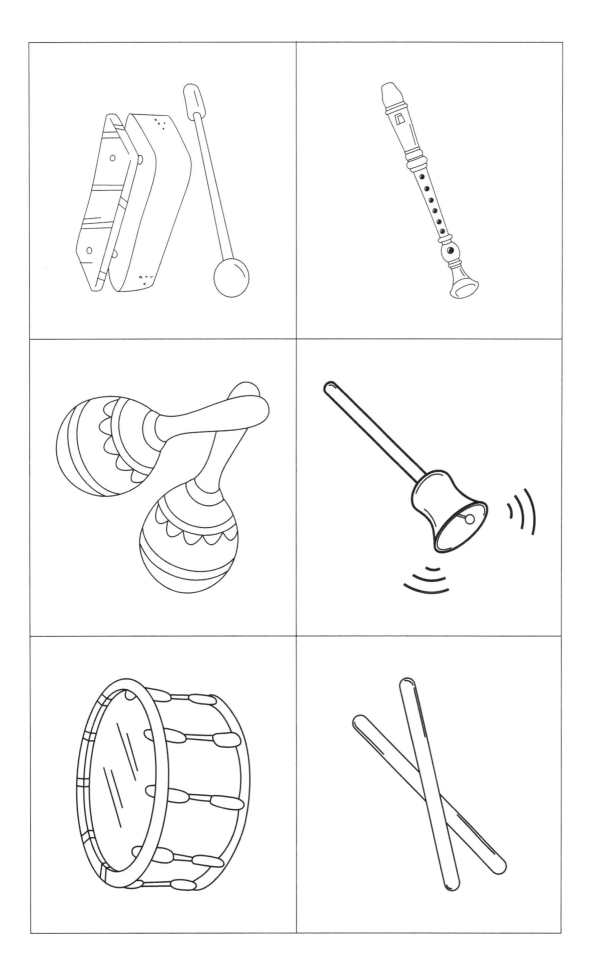

Section 13: Sounds, Sound Makers and Musical Instruments

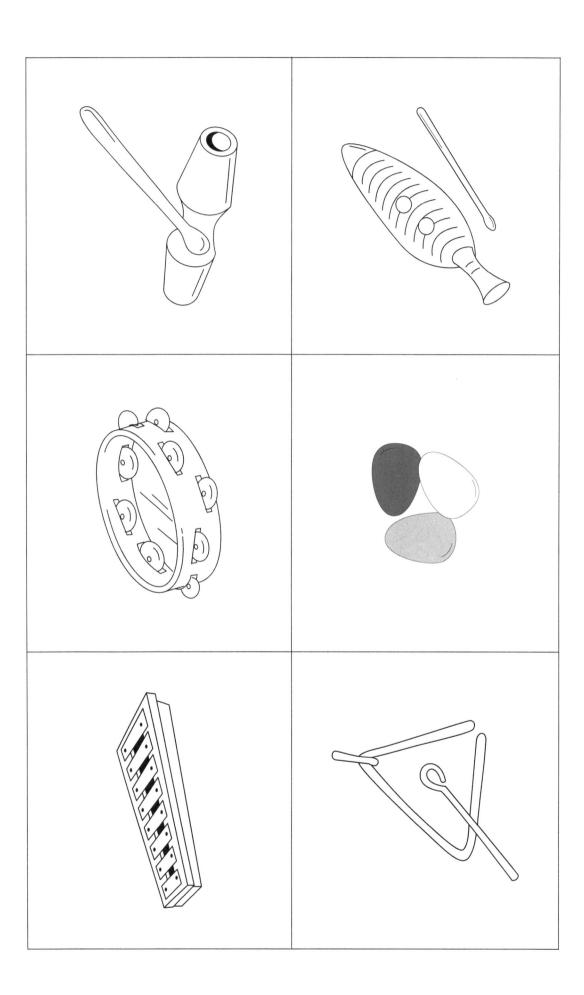

Section 13: Sounds, Sound Makers and Musical Instruments

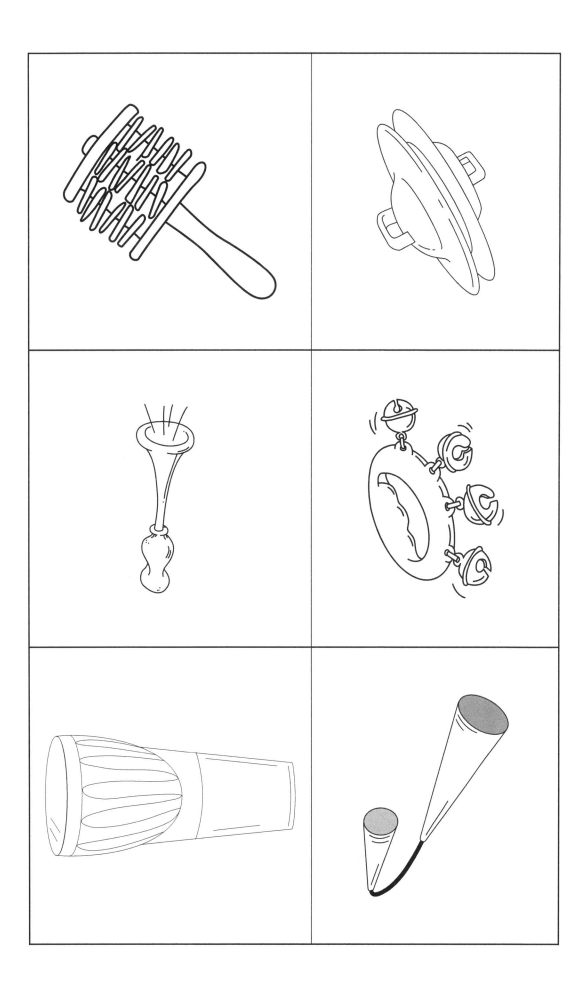

Section 13: Sounds, Sound Makers and Musical Instruments

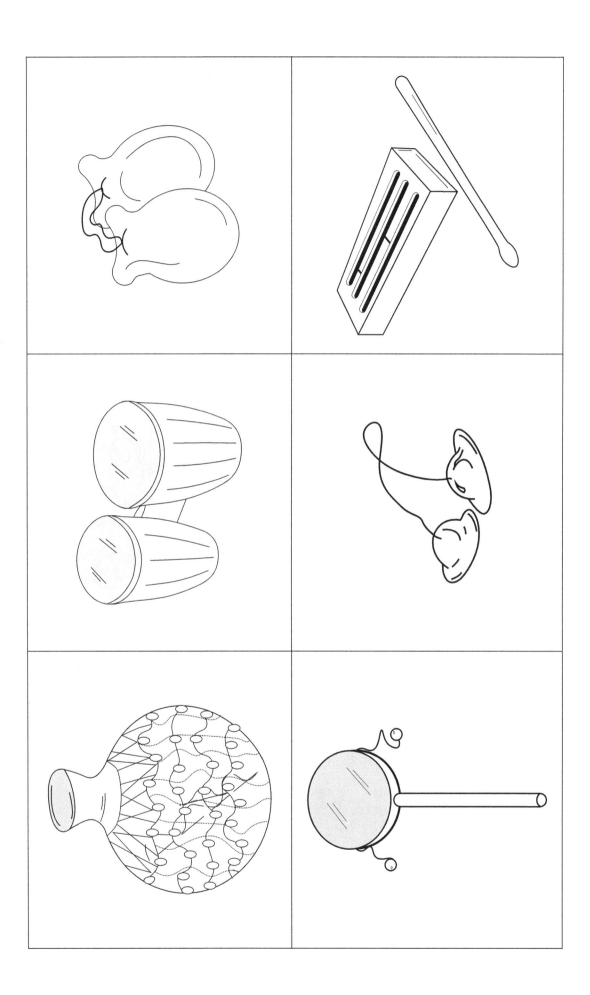

SOUNDS, SOUND MAKERS AND MUSICAL INSTRUMENTS
Homemade Instruments

- ❑ bell – tap a suspended clay pot with a stick
- ❑ castanets – bang two plastic egg cups together
- ❑ cymbals – bang two saucepan lids together
- ❑ drum – empty biscuit tin/large cardboard box and a wooden spoon
- ❑ gong – frying pan or saucepan lid suspended by cord
- ❑ kazoo – blow on tissue paper wrapped round a comb
- ❑ rhythm sticks – cut up a dowel stick (sand edges to round off and remove splinters)
- ❑ tone instruments – tap bottles filled with different amounts of water with a stick
- ❑ trumpet – bend a piece of cardboard into a cone shape
- ❑ guiro – plastic bottle with ridges and a stick

SOUNDS, SOUND MAKERS AND MUSICAL INSTRUMENTS
Shakers

Make shakers by collecting everyday objects to place in different containers. It is important that the lid can be placed on the container *securely:* otherwise objects may fly out and cause injury.

Any of the following can be used to make a shaker:

- ❏ jars
- ❏ plastic storage jars
- ❏ margarine and yogurt pots
- ❏ plastic bottles
- ❏ small boxes
- ❏ tins

Sound makers for shakers

- ❏ beads
- ❏ buttons
- ❏ wooden bricks
- ❏ sand
- ❏ dried foods (rice/pasta/beans)
- ❏ paper strips (use thin cardboard)

- ❏ small stones/pebbles
- ❏ cotton reels
- ❏ small toys
- ❏ keys
- ❏ pegs
- ❏ curtain hooks
- ❏ crayons

Always be extremely careful with small objects, which may be swallowed accidentally by young children. Items should be placed in shakers with *secure* lids. If in any doubt, use larger objects or toys.

SOUNDS, SOUND MAKERS AND MUSICAL INSTRUMENTS
Home Sounds

- ☐ phone
- ☐ vacuum cleaner
- ☐ washing machine
- ☐ fridge
- ☐ water running
- ☐ bath time
- ☐ cooking sounds
- ☐ talking
- ☐ laughter
- ☐ baby gurgling/crying
- ☐ doorbell
- ☐ music

- ☐ television
- ☐ doors banging
- ☐ door knocker
- ☐ alarm clock
- ☐ crockery chinking
- ☐ footsteps
- ☐ pet noises, e.g. barking, mewing
- ☐ cleaning sounds, sweeping, rubbing
- ☐ lawn mower
- ☐ hedge clipper

SOUNDS, SOUND MAKERS AND MUSICAL INSTRUMENTS
Human Sounds

- ☐ laughter
- ☐ crying
- ☐ shouting
- ☐ talking
- ☐ whispering
- ☐ voices with different emotions, e.g. anger, surprise
- ☐ informal speech (friends chatting)
- ☐ formal speech (news reader)
- ☐ screaming
- ☐ yawning
- ☐ tut-tut

- ☐ exclamations: oh! mmm! ah! sh!
- ☐ sneezing
- ☐ coughing
- ☐ moan of pain
- ☐ brushing hair
- ☐ washing face or hands
- ☐ cleaning teeth
- ☐ washing hair
- ☐ dressing
- ☐ bathing
- ☐ showering

Symbolic sounds

- ☐ slide – whee!
- ☐ roundabout – whee!
- ☐ bus – beep-beep; ding-ding; vroom!
- ☐ car – beep-beep; vroom!
- ☐ train – choo-choo; chchch-choo

- ☐ clock – tick-tock
- ☐ telephone – dring-dring
- ☐ cat – miaow!
- ☐ tiger – rarrgh!

SOUNDS, SOUND MAKERS AND MUSICAL INSTRUMENTS
Animal Sounds

Farm

- ☐ cow – moo
- ☐ pig – oink
- ☐ sheep – baa
- ☐ dog – woof-woof
- ☐ cat – miaow
- ☐ cockerel – cock-a-doodle-doo

- ☐ cuckoo – cuckoo
- ☐ chicken – cluck
- ☐ duck – quack-quack
- ☐ horse – neigh
- ☐ bird – tweet

Zoo

- ☐ elephant – trumpet
- ☐ lion – roar
- ☐ tiger—rarrgh

- ☐ birds – tweet; whistle; chirp
- ☐ monkey – oo-oo
- ☐ bear – grrrr

Pets

- ☐ cat – miaow; purr
- ☐ dog – woof-woof
- ☐ parrot – squawk

- ☐ budgie – tweet; chirp
- ☐ mouse – squeak; eek-eek

SOUNDS, SOUND MAKERS AND MUSICAL INSTRUMENTS
Environmental Sounds

Garden

- ☐ lawn mower
- ☐ hedge trimmer
- ☐ birds
- ☐ bees
- ☐ plants being watered
- ☐ sweeping
- ☐ digging
- ☐ people laughing
- ☐ drinks being poured
- ☐ cooking on the barbecue
- ☐ water in a fountain
- ☐ children playing

Street

- ☐ traffic
- ☐ car horns
- ☐ train
- ☐ aeroplane
- ☐ sirens
- ☐ newspaper man
- ☐ road works
- ☐ bus bell
- ☐ car screeching
- ☐ people talking
- ☐ stall holders
- ☐ street entertainers
- ☐ pedestrian signal

Weather

- ☐ wind
- ☐ hailstones
- ☐ rain (different types)
- ☐ thunder
- ☐ lightening

Section 13: Sounds, Sound Makers and Musical Instruments

School

- playground bell
- whistle
- chairs scraping
- musical instruments
- beeps on computer
- children laughing
- voice of teacher
- doors banging
- windows banging
- piano
- singing
- skipping
- football
- children playing, e.g. toy bricks dropping
- dinner plates
- cutlery
- playground noises, such as games, skipping songs
- assembly
- story time
- sound of feet
- books shutting or dropping
- scissors cutting paper
- pencil being sharpened
- pencil scribbling
- fingers tapping on a window or table

Transport

- aeroplane
- train
- underground train
- bus, e.g. horn, bell
- car engine
- car horn
- motorbike
- bike bell
- wheels on a skateboard
- ship's hooter

Farm

- tractor
- animal sounds
- talking
- shouting
- milk churns
- lorry

Section 13: Sounds, Sound Makers and Musical Instruments

Zoo

- ice-cream seller
- crowd sounds
- animal sounds
- feeding time, e.g. calling to animals, noise of the feeding bucket
- noise of animals moving or swimming
- cafeteria
- cashier

Shops

- crowd sounds
- announcements
- lift bell
- arguments
- trolley
- tins falling
- piped music

Railway station

- announcements
- people talking
- guard shouting
- flower seller
- crowd noises
- buffet bar
- ticket machine
- train noises
- doors opening and closing

Swimming pool

- water splashing
- locker door opening and closing
- change machine
- bell
- children shouting

SOUNDS, SOUND MAKERS AND MUSICAL INSTRUMENTS
Action Sounds

- ☐ clapping
- ☐ stamping
- ☐ dancing
- ☐ skipping
- ☐ rubbing hands together
- ☐ tapping fingers in palm
- ☐ running

- ☐ walking
- ☐ banging
- ☐ clicking fingers
- ☐ drumming fingers
- ☐ sliding feet
- ☐ tapping foot
- ☐ knocking or banging

APPENDIX I
Record Sheet

Appendix I

Child's name:

Date	Activity/Context	Observations

AI = adult initiated activity; CI = child initiated activity

APPENDIX II
Further Reading

Burke, Nicola (2018) *Musical Development Matters in the Early Years (EYFS)* Early Education: Watford. www.early-education.org.uk

Department for Education (2019) *Early Years Foundation Stage Profile 2019 handbook,* www.gov.uk/government/publications/early-years-foundation-stage-profile-handbook

Department for Education (2017) *Statutory Framework for the Early Years Foundation Stage,* www.gov.uk/government/publications/early-years-foundation-stage-framework--2

Knowles, W. and Masidlover, M. (2018) *The Derbyshire Language Scheme,* www.derbyshire-language-scheme.co.uk

Moylett, Helen and Stewart, Nancy (2012) *Development Matters in the Early Years Foundation Stage (EYFS),* Early Education: Watford. www.early-education.org.uk

National Deaf Children's Society (2015) *How To Make Music Activities Accessible For Deaf Children And Young People,* National Deaf Children's Society: London.

National Deaf Children's Society (2015) *Supporting The Achievement Of Deaf Children In Early Years Settings,* National Deaf Children's Society: London.

National Deaf Children's Society (2019) *Supporting The Achievement Of Deaf Children Who Use English As An Additional Language (EAL),* National Deaf Children's Society: London.

Williams, D. (2019) *Early Visual Skills: A Resource for Working with Children with Under-Developed Visual Perceptual Skills,* Routledge: Abingdon, Oxon.

APPENDIX III
Resources

Toys, materials and equipment are available from the following companies:

United Kingdom

Consortium
Hammond Way
Trowbridge
Wiltshire   BA14 8RR
www.consortiumeducation.com

Early Learning Centre
Cherry Tree Road
Watford
Hertfordshire   WD24 6SH
www.elc.co.uk

Hope Education
2 Gregory Street
Hyde
Cheshire   SK14 4TH
www.hope-education.co.uk

LDA
2 Gregory Street
Hyde
Cheshire   SK14 4TH
www.ldalearning.com

Sensory Education Limited
310–314 Summer Lane
Birmingham   B19 3RH
www.cheapdisabilityaids.co.uk

Speechmark
Routledge | Taylor & Francis Group
2–4 Park Square
Milton Park
Abingdon
Oxon   OX14 4RN
www.routledge.com

Taskmaster
Arkwright Road
Bicester
Oxon   OX26 4UU
www.taskmasteronline.co.uk

TFH
Sensory Toys and Special Needs
Toy specialists
Unit 5–7 Severnside Business Park
Severn Road
Stourport-on-Severn
Worcestershire   DY13 9HT
www.specialneedstoys.com/uk/

Winslow Resources
Goyt Side Road
Chesterfield
Derbyshire   S40 2PH
www.winslowresources.com

United States of America

Didax Inc
395 Main Street
Rowley   MA 01969
www.didax.com

S&S Worldwide
75 Mill Street
PO Box 515
Colchester   CT 06415
www.ssww.com

TFH USA Ltd.
4537 Gibsonia Road
Gibsonia   PA 15044
www.specialneedstoys.com/usa/